Sr

Bhag

GIT

Ramesh Menon was born in 1951 in New Delhi. He has also written modern renderings of the Mahabharata, Ramayana, Srimad Bhagavad Gita, Siva Purana, Devi Purana and Bhagavata Purana.

From the same author:

The Mahabharata: A Modern Rendering
Devi: The Devi Bhagavatam Retold
Siva: The Siva Purana Retold
Bhagavata Purana
Adi Parva
Krishna: Life and Song of the Blue God

Srimad Bhagavad GITA

Ramesh Menon

RUPA

Published by
Rupa Publications India Pvt. Ltd 2007
7/16, Ansari Road, Daryaganj
New Delhi 110002

Sales centres:
Allahabad Bengaluru Chennai
Hyderabad Jaipur Kathmandu
Kolkata Mumbai

ISBN: 978-81-291-1447-1

Sixth impression 2021

10 9 8 7 6

Typeset in 12 Nalandabas by Mindways Design, New Delhi

Printed at Saurabh Printers Pvt. Ltd, Noida

In memory of my grandfather,
K.R.K. Menon

INTRODUCTION

My focus while translating the Song of God, of which there are already so many fine translations, was to remain as rigorously faithful to the original as I could, without compromising its poetry. I have deliberately tried to preserve the Sanskrit order of words, as far as possible, and also not to use any words or phrases which do not appear in the Sanskrit.

I hope that this brings a certain immediacy and directness (more than explanation) to the translation.

It is worth remembering that this Scripture belongs to another age, (the dwapara yuga), and was expounded not just to anyone but to Arjuna, the son of a deva and greatest kshatriya warrior of that time, between two vast armies, on the brink of a dharma yuddha, a war for truth.

However, I believe that the Bhagavad Gita contains the voice of God and that it speaks to each of us, to every mind and heart—individually. This intimate communion transcends the merely intellectual: *sarvaśah,* in every way.

Also, mine is a bhakta, a devotee's, translation, because this most Holy Book, which I first discovered almost forty years ago, did change my life and continues to do so.

canto 1

the despair of arjuna

1

dhṛtarāṣṭra uvāca
dharmakṣetre kurukṣetre
samavetā yuyutsavaḥ
māmakāḥ pāṇḍavāś cai'va
kim akurvata saṁjaya

2

saṁjaya uvāca
dṛṣṭvā tu pāṇḍavānīkaṁ
vyūḍhaṁ duryodhanas tadā
ācāryam upasaṁgamya
rājā vacanam abravīt

3

paśyai'tāṁ pāṇḍuputrāṇām
ācārya mahatīṁ camūm
vyūḍhāṁ drupadaputreṇa
tava śiṣyeṇa dhīmatā

4

atra śūrā maheṣvāsā
bhīmārjunasamā yudhi
yuyudhāno virāṭaś ca
drupadaś ca mahārathaḥ

5

dhṛṣṭaketuś cekitānaḥ
kāśirājaś ca vīryavān
purujit kuntibhojaś ca
śaibyaś ca narapuṁgavaḥ

1

dhritarashtra said:
upon the field of dharma,* field of kuru,
gathered keened for war,
my force and the sons of pandu, what did they do,
sanjaya?

2

sanjaya said:
seeing the pandava army arrayed, duryodhana then
his honoured master approached; the king said these
words:

3

behold, this immense army, master, of the sons of
pandu,
deployed by drupada's son, your brilliant pupil.

4

here, heroes, mighty bowmen, of bheema and arjuna
equals in war—
yuyudhana and virata, and drupada maharatha;**

5

dhrishtaketu, chekitana, and the valiant kasiraja,
purujit and kuntibhoja, and the shaibya, bull among
men.

---

*truth; righteousness.

**great chariot warrior.

6

yudhamanyuś ca vikrānta
uttamaujāś ca vīryavān
saubhadro draupadeyāś ca
sarva eva mahārathāḥ

7

asmākaṁ tu viśiṣṭā ye
tān nibodha dvijottama
nāyakā mama sainyasya
saṁjñārthaṁ tān bravīmi te

8

bhavān bhīṣmaś ca karṇaś ca
kṛpaś ca samitiṁjayaḥ
aśvatthāmā vikarṇaś ca
saumadattis tathai 'va ca

9

anye ca bahavah śūrā
madarthe tyaktajīvitāh
nānāśastrapraharaṇāḥ
sarve yuddhaviśāradāḥ

10

aparyāptaṁ tad asmākaṃ
balaṁ bhīṣmābhirakṣitam
paryāptaṁ tv idam eteṣāṁ
balaṁ bhīmābhirakṣitam

6

and yuddhamanyu the brave and the intrepid uttamaujas,
subhadra's son† and draupadi's princes—surely, maharathas all.

7

be aware, also, of the distinguished amongst us, o best of dvijas,* the commanders of my army—let me name them for you to know.

8

yourself and bheeshma and karna, and kripa winner of wars; asvatthama and vikarna, and the son of somadatta, as well.

9

and so many other heroes, too, willing to give their lives for me;
myriad weapons they wield, all of them masters of war.

10

our army is invincible, defended comprehensively by the might of bheeshma;
their force is inferior, guarded by bheema's strength all around.

---

†abhimanyu.

*the twice-born, the two upper castes; in this case, the brahmanas.

11

ayaneṣu ca sarveṣu
yathābhāgam avasthitāḥ
bhīṣmam evā 'bhirakṣantu
bhavantaḥ sarva eva hi

12

tasya saṁjanayan harṣaṁ
kuruvṛddhaḥ pitāmahaḥ
siṁhanâdaṁ vinadyo 'ccaiḥ
śaṅkhaṁ dadhmau pratāpavān

13

tataḥ śaṅkhāś ca bheryaś ca
paṇavānakagomukhāḥ
sahasai 'vā 'bhyahanyanta
sa śabdas tumulo 'bhavat

14

tataḥ śvetair hayair yukte
mahati syandane sthitau
mādhavaḥ pāṇḍavaś cai 'va
divyau śaṅkhau pradadhmatuḥ

15

pāñcajanyaṁ hṛṣīkeśo
devadattaṁ dhanaṁjayaḥ
pauṇḍraṁ dadhmau mahāśaṅkhaṁ
bhīmakarmā vṛkodaraḥ

11

and positioned at every ingress, each at your station,
bheeshma alone you must all perfectly protect, surely,
from every side.

12

to hearten him, the mighty kuru ancient,* the grandsire,
a lion's roar let out and blew his conch reverberantly.

13

then, conches and bugles and trumpets, kettledrums, horns
resounded suddenly, all together: that sound was tumultuary.

14

when, from a magnificent chariot, white horses yoked to it,
madhava†† and the pandava,† also, their divine conches sounded.

15

the panchajanya, hrishikesa;‡ the devadatta, dhananjaya;#
the great conch paundra, blew vrikodara** of awesome deeds.

---

*bheeshma.

††krishna.

†arjuna.

‡krishna; vishnu.

#arjuna; lit. 'winner of wealth'.

**bheema; lit. 'wolf-belly'.

16

anantavijayaṁ rājā
kuntīputro yudhiṣṭhiraḥ
nakulaḥ sahadevaś ca
sughoṣamaṇipuṣpakau

17

kāśyaś ca parameṣvāsaḥ
śikhaṇḍī ca mahārathaḥ
dhṛṣṭadyumno virāṭaś ca
sātyakiś cā parājitaḥ

18

drupado draupadeyāś ca
sarvaśah pṛthivīpate
saubhadraś ca mahābāhuḥ
śaṅkhān dadhmuḥ pṛthak-pṛthak

19

sa ghoṣo dhārtarāṣṭrāṇāṁ
hṛdayāni vyadārayat
nabhaś ca pṛthivīṁ cai 'va
tumulo vyanunādayan

20

atha vyavasthitān dṛṣṭvā
dhārtārāṣṭrān kapidhvajaḥ
pravṛtte śastrasaṁpāte
dhanur udyamya pāṇḍavaḥ

16

the anantavijayam, the king, kunti's son, yudhishtira;
nakula and sahadeva: the sughosha, the manipushpaka.

17

and the kaasi, supreme archer, and shikhandi,
maharatha; dhrishtadyumna and virata and satyaki, the unvanquished.

18

drupada and all the sons of draupadi, o lord of the earth,
and subhadra's mighty-armed son sounded their conches, every one.

19

that clamour dhritarashtra's sons' hearts pierced;
and sky and earth, also, that fierce uproar shook.

20

now, watching in formation the sons of dhritarashtra,
the monkey-bannered* pandava, when weapons were about to be loosed, raised his bow.

---

*hanuman.

21

hṛṣīkeśaṁ tadā vākyam
idam āha mahīpate
arjuna uvāca
senayor ubhayor madhye
rathaṁ sthāpaya me 'cyuta

22

yāvad etān nirīkṣe 'haṁ
yoddhukāmān avasthitān
kair mayā saha yoddhavyam
asmin raṇasamudyame

23

yotsyamānān avekṣe 'haṁ
ya ete 'tra samāgatāḥ
dhārtarāṣṭrasya durbuddher
yuddhe priyacikīrṣavaḥ

24

saṁjaya uvāca evam ukto hṛṣīkeśo
guḍākeśena bhārata
senayor ubhayor madhye
sthāpayitvā rathottamam

25

bhīṣmadroṇapramukhataḥ
sarveṣāṁ ca mahīkṣitām
uvāca pārtha paśyai 'tān
samavetān kurūn iti

21

then, to hrishikesa he spoke these words, lord of the earth:
arjuna said: between the two armies, set my chariot, achyuta.†

22

so i can look at those arrayed against us, seeking war,
against whom i must fight—before battle begins.

23

the warriors let me see, that have come together here,
wanting to please dhritarashtra's evil-minded son with war.

24

sanjaya said:
asked this by gudakesa,* hrishikesa, o bhaarata,††
drawing up that fine chariot between the two armies,

25

before bheeshma, drona and all the rulers of the earth,
said, 'partha,** look at these massed kurus.'

---

†krishna; immaculate one.

*arjuna; curly-haired; conqueror of sleep.

††dhritarashtra is a descendant of the ancient king bharata, after whom bharata varsha is named.

**arjuna; pritha's (kunti) son.

26

tatrā 'paśyat sthitān pārthaḥ
pitṝn atha pitāmahān
ācāryān mātulān bhrātṝn
putrān pautrān sakhīṁs tathā

27

śvaśurān suhṛdaś cai 'va
senayor ubhayor api
tān samīkṣya sa kaunteyaḥ
sarvān bandhūn avasthitān

28

kṛpayā parayā 'viṣṭo
viṣīdann idam abravīt
arjuna uvāca
dṛṣṭve 'maṁ svajanaṁ kṛṣṇa
yuyutsuṁ samupasthitam

29

sīdanti mama gātrāṇi
mukhaṁ ca pariśuṣyati
vepathuś ca śarīre me
romaharṣaś ca jāyate

30

gāṇḍīvaṁ sraṁsate hastāt
tvak cai 'va paridahyate
na ca śaknomy avasthātuṁ
bhramatī 'va ca me manaḥ

26

then partha saw standing there fathers and grandfathers, masters, uncles,† brothers, sons, grandsons and friends,

27

fathers-in-law and well-wishers—and in both armies, besides; the son of kunti looked closely at all those kinsmen deployed.

28

by great pity overcome, stricken, he said this:
arjuna said:
i see my kinsmen, krishna, gathered avid for war.

29

my limbs turn weak, my mouth is parched;
and my body trembles, and my hair stands on end.

30

the gandiva slips from my hands and my skin burns;
and my anxiety i cannot control and the fierce whirling of my mind;

---

†maternal.

31

nimittāni ca paśyāmi
viparītāni keśava
na ca śreyo 'nupaśyāmi
hatvā svajanam āhave

32

na kāṅkṣe vijayaṁ kṛṣṇa
na ca rājyaṁ sukhāni ca
kiṁ no rājyena govinda
kiṁ bhogair jīvitena vā

33

yeṣām arthe kāṅkṣitaṁ no
rājyaṁ bhogāḥ sukhāni ca
ta ime 'vasthitā yuddhe
prāṇāṁs tyaktvā dhanāni ca

34

ācāryāh pitaraḥ putrās
tathai 'va ca pitāmahāḥ
mātulāḥ śvaśurāḥ pautrāḥ
śyālāḥ saṁbandhinas tathā

35

etān na hantum icchāmi
ghnato 'pi madhusūdana
api trailokyārajyasya
hetoḥ kiṁ nu mahīkṛte

31

and omens i see, evil, kesava,
and nor do i see what good can come from killing my kinsmen in battle.

32

i do not want victory, krishna, neither kingdom nor happiness;
for what a kingdom, govinda, what for pleasures or even life?

33

those for whose sake we want a kingdom, pleasures or happiness,
they are here for war, leaving their lives and wealth.

34

masters, fathers, sons, and grandsires, too;
uncles, fathers-in-law, grandsons, brothers-in-law and other kinsmen;

35

i do not want to kill them even if they kill me, madhusudana:*
not for lordship over the three worlds,† what then of this earth?

---

*krishna, slayer of the demon madhu.

†svarga, bhumi and patala; heaven, earth and the under-world.

36

nihatya dhārtarāṣṭrān naḥ
kā prītiḥ syāj janārdana
pāpam evā 'śrayed asmān
hatvai 'tān ātatāyinaḥ

37

tasmān nā 'rhā vayaṁ hantuṁ
dhārtarāṣṭrān svabāndhavān
svajanaṁ hi kathaṁ hatvā
sukhinaḥ syāma mādhava

38

yady apy ete na paśyanti
lobho pahatacetasaḥ
kulakṣayakṛtaṁ doṣaṁ
mitradrohe ca pātakam

39

kathaṁ na jñeyam asmābhiḥ
pāpād asmān nivartitum
kulakṣayakṛtaṁ doṣaṁ
prapaśyadbhir janārdana

40

kulakṣaye praṇaśyanti
kuladharmāḥ sanātanāḥ
dharme naṣṭe kulaṁ kṛtsnam
adharmo 'bhibhavaty uta

36

killing dhritarashtra's sons, what joy will we get, janardana?‡
we will only find sin ourselves if we slay these sinners.

37

so, we must not kill the sons of dhritarashtra, who are our kin; for, after killing our own, how can we be happy, madhava?*

38

even if these, their hearts ruined by greed, see no atrocity in destroying the clan and no crime in harming friends,

39

why don't we realise that we must desist from this sin, when we see clearly how heinous it is to exterminate one's race, janardana?

40

with the destruction of the clan, ancient family traditions are lost forever;
when dharma is no more, evil takes all that race.

---

‡krishna.
*krishna.

41

adharmābhibhavāt kṛṣṇa
praduṣyanti kulastriyaḥ
strīṣu duṣṭāsu vārṣṇeya
jāyate varṇasaṁkaraḥ

42

saṁkaro narakāyai 'va
kulaghnānāṁ kulasya ca
patanti pitaro hy eṣāṁ
luptapiṇḍodakakriyāḥ

43

doṣair etaiḥ kulaghnānāṁ
varṇasaṁkarakārakaiḥ
utsādyante jātidharmāḥ
kuladharmāś ca śāśvatāḥ

44

utsannakuladharmāṇāṁ
manuṣyāṇāṁ janārdana
narake niyataṁ vāso
bhavatī 'ty anuśuśruma

45

aho bata mahat pāpaṁ
kartuṁ vyavasitā vayam
yad rājyasukhalobhena
hantuṁ svajanam udyatāḥ

41
when adharma rules, krishna, the women of the clan become loose;
when the women are depraved, vaarshaneya,* the varnas† become mixed.

42
crossbreeding only casts into hell those that ruin the clan, and the clan, itself;
their manes surely fall, for the ritual of the offering of rice-balls and holy water having disappeared.

43
through the sins of these clan-destroyers, defilers of the varnas,
lost are sacred traditions** of caste and family, forever.

44
men whose kuladharma has been destroyed, janardana, will live forever in hell, as i have heard.

45
ah, what a great sin we have decided to commit:
that from greed for the pleasures of kingdom, we are ready to kill our kinsmen.

*krishna, scion of the vrishnis.
†castes.
**dharma, spiritual.

46

yadi mām apratīkāram
aśastraṁ śastrapāṇayaḥ
dhārtarāṣṭrā raṇe hanyus
tan me kṣemataraṁ bhavet

47

saṁjaya uvāca
evam uktvā 'rjunah saṁkhye
rathopastha upāviśat
visṛjya saśaraṁ cāpaṁ
śokasaṁvignamānasaḥ

46

while i am unarmed and unresisting,
let dhritarashtra's sons kill me on the field of war—that i could still bear.

47

sanjaya said:
saying this, arjuna sat down in the back of that chariot, in war;
he cast aside his arrows and bow, his heart plunged in profound anguish.

this is the first canto of the srimad bhagavad gita named arjuna vishada yoga

canto 2

*the way of samkhya**

*see appendix.

1

saṁjaya uvāca
taṁ tathā kṛpayā 'viṣṭam
aśrupūrṇākulekṣaṇam
viṣīdantam idaṁ vākyam
uvāca madhusūdanaḥ

2

śrībhagavān uvāca
kutas tvā kaśmalam idaṁ
viṣame samupasthitam
anāryajuṣṭam asvargyam
akīrtikaram arjuna

3

klaibyaṁ mā sma gamaḥ pārtha
nai 'tat tvayy upapadyate
kṣudraṁ hṛdayadaurbalyaṁ
tyaktvo 'ttiṣṭha paraṁtapa

4

arjuna uvāca
kathaṁ bhīṣmam ahaṁ saṁkhye
droṇaṁ ca madhusūdana
iṣubhiḥ pratiyotsyāmi
pūjārhāv arisūdana

5

gurūn ahatvā hi mahānubhāvān
śreyo bhoktuṁ bhaikṣyam apī 'ha loke
hatvā 'rthakāmāṁs tu gurūn ithai 'va
bhuñjīya bhogān rudhirapradigdhān

1

sanjaya said:

seeing him so, in the grip of pity, tearful, agitated,
griefstricken, these words to him spoke madhusudana.

2

the gracious lord said:

from where has this stain come over you at this critical time? this is the way of the base; it does not lead to heaven but fetches infamy, arjuna.

3

do not go this cowardly way, partha; it is beneath you; abandon this vile faint-heartedness, and arise, o bane of your enemies!

4

arjuna said: how will i attack bheeshma and drona in battle, madhusudana,
with arrows, when they are worthy of worship, arisudana?*

5

surely, without killing one's masters and noble elders, it is better to live by begging alms in this world;
else, by killing our masters, if we enjoy wealth and pleasures we shall enjoy blood-stained spoils.

---

*slayer of enemies.

6

na cai 'tad vidmaḥ kataran no garīyo
yad vā jayema yadi vā no jayeyuḥ
yān eva hatvā na jijīviṣāmas
te 'vasthitāh pramukhe dhārtarāṣṭrāḥ

7

kārpaṇyadoṣopahatasvabhāvaḥ
pṛcchāmi tvāṁ dharmasaṁmūḍhacetāḥ
yac chreyaḥ syān niścitaṁ brūhi tan me
śiṣyas te 'haṁ śādhi māṁ tvāṁ prapannam

8

na hi prapaśyāmi mamā 'panudyād
yac chokam ucchoṣaṇam indriyāṇām
avāpya bhūmāv asapatnam ṛddhaṁ
rājyaṁ surāṇām api cā 'dhipatyam

9

saṁjaya uvāca
evam uktvā hṛṣīkeśaṁ
guḍākeśaḥ paraṁtapaḥ
na yotsya iti govindam
uktvā tūṣṇīṁ babhūva ha

10

tam uvāca hṛṣīkeśaḥ
prahasann iva bhārata
senayor ubhayor madhye
viṣīdantam idaṁ vacaḥ

6

we do not know which of these would be better for us:
that we conquer them or that they vanquish us!
they whom killing, we would not wish to live—standing
before us, the sons of dhritarashtra.

7

the weakness of pity besieges my nature; my mind
confounded about what dharma is, i ask you—
tell me what is unquestionably best for me. i am your
disciple; teach me, i submit to you.

8

because i cannot see what can exorcise this anguish that
withers my senses,
not if i gained a thriving and unrivalled kingdom on
earth, and even lordship over the gods of light.*

9

sanjaya said:
speaking thus to hrishikesa, gudakesa, scourge of his
enemies,
said 'i will not fight' and fell silent.

10

then, hrishikesa spoke smilingly, bhaarata,
between two armies, to him who sorrowed, these words.

---

*the devas.

11

śrībhagavān uvāca

aśocyān anvaśocas tvaṁ
prajñāvādāṁś ca bhāṣase
gatāsūn agatāsūṁś ca
nā 'nuśocanti paṇḍitāḥ

12

na tv evā 'haṁ jātu nā 'saṁ
na tvaṁ ne 'me janādhipāḥ
na cai 'va na bhaviṣyāmaḥ
sarve vayam ataḥ param

13

dehino 'smin yathā dehe
kaumāraṁ yauvanaṁ jarā
tathā dehāntaraprāptir
dhīras tatra na muhyati

14

mātrāsparśās tu kaunteya
śītoṣṇasukhaduḥkhadāḥ
āgamā pāyino 'nityās
tāṁs titikṣasva bhārata

15

yaṁ hi na vyathayanty ete
puruṣaṁ puruṣarṣabha
samaduḥkhasukhaṁ dhīraṁ
so 'mṛtatvāya kalpate

11

the gracious lord said:
you grieve for those not worth grieving over, and argue as if you were a wise man discoursing;
not for the dead or for the living do the wise grieve.

12

surely, at no time ever did i not exist, or you, or all these kings;
and for sure, not in any future to come will any of us cease to exist.

13

just as the indweller passes, in the body,
through childhood, youth and old age,
the soul also assumes new bodies;
the wise are not perplexed by this.

14

contact between the elements alone, son of kunti,
causes cold and heat, pleasure and pain;
these come and go, they are evanescent; endure them, bhaarata.

15

whom these cannot perturb, the wise man, o bull among men;
who is the same in sorrow and joy, steadfast, is fit for immortality.

16

nā 'sato vidyate bhāvo
nā 'bhāvo vidyate sataḥ
ubhayor api dṛṣṭo 'ntas tv
anayos tattvadarśibhiḥ

17

avināśi tu tad vidhi
yena sarvam idaṁ tatam
vināśam avyayasyā 'sya
na kaścit kartum arhati

18

antavanta ime dehā
nityasyo 'ktāḥ śarīriṇaḥ
anāśino 'prameyasya
tasmād yudhyasva bhārata

19

ya enaṁ vetti hantāraṁ
yaś cai 'naṁ manyate hatam
ubhau tau na vijānīto
nā 'yaṁ hanti na hanyate

20

na jāyate mriyate vā kadācin
nā 'yaṁ bhūtvā bhavitā vā na bhūyaḥ
ajo nityaḥ śāśvato 'yaṁ purāṇo
na hanyate hanyamāne śarīre

16
never does the unreal exist, and the real never ceases to be; of both these, surely, the end has been seen by seers of truth.

17
but, know, what pervades all this is immortal;
that everlasting *being* no one can destroy.

18
mortal these bodies; eternal, it is said, the embodied soul;
it is immortal, ineffable—so, fight bhaarata!

19
he that thinks of it as being a killer and he who thinks *this* is slain:
both do not know—it neither kills nor is slain.

20
this is not born nor ever dies, not in the past, present or future;
un-born, changeless, eternal it is, primeval; it is not killed when the body is slain.

21

vedā 'vināśinaṁ nityaṁ
ya enam ajam avyayam
kathaṁ sa puruṣaḥ pārtha
kaṁ ghātayati hanti kam

22

vāsāṁsi jīrṇāni yathā vihāya
navāni gṛhṇāti naro 'parāṇi
tathā śarīrāṇi vihāya jīrṇāny
anyāni saṁyāti navāni dehī

23

nai 'naṁ chindanti śastrāṇi
nai 'naṁ dahati pāvakaḥ
na cai 'naṁ kledayanty āpo
na śoṣayati mārutaḥ

24

acchedyo 'yam adāhyo 'yam
akledyo 'śoṣya eva ca
nityaḥ sarvagataḥ sthāṇur
acalo 'yaṁ sanātanaḥ

25

avyakto 'yam acintyo 'yam
avikāryo 'yam ucyate
tasmād evaṁ viditvai 'naṁ
nā 'nuśocitum arhasi

21

knowing this is indestructible, constant, un-born, immutable, how does a man kill anyone, partha, who does he kill?

22

even as a man abandons old, tattered clothes and puts on other fresh ones,
the indweller leaves old, worn bodies and enters other new ones.

23

weapons cannot pierce it; fire cannot burn it;
water does not wet it, nor dry it, the wind.

24

not pierceable, not burnable, not wettable, and also not dryable—
permanent, ubiquitous, abiding, invariable, eternal.

25

unmanifest, *it*; inconceivable, it; changeless, it, they say;
so, knowing it is such, you must not despair.

26

atha cai 'naṁ nityajātaṁ
nityaṁ vā manyase mṛtam
tathā 'pi tvaṁ mahābāho
nai 'naṁ śocitum arhasi

27

jātasya hi dhruvo mṛtyur
dhruvaṁ janma mṛtasya ca
tasmād aparihārye 'rthe
na tvaṁ śocitum arhasi

28

avyaktādīni bhūtāni
vyaktamadhyāni bhārata
avyaktanidhanāny eva
tatra kā paridevanā

29

āścaryavat paśyati kaścid enam
āścaryavad vadati tathai 'va cā 'nyaḥ
āścaryavac cai 'nam anyaḥ śṛṇoti
śrutvā 'py enaṁ veda na cai 'va kaścit

30

dehī nityam avadhyo 'yaṁ
dehe sarvasya bhārata
tasmāt sarvāṇi bhūtāni
na tvaṁ śocitum arhasi

26

and if you think that it is constantly being born and continually dying,
even then, mighty-armed, you ought not to despair.

27

for he who is born death is certain, and birth is certain for who dies;
so, over what you believe to be ineluctable, you should not despair.

28

unmanifest the source of beings, manifest their interim, bhaarata;
unmanifest, too, their end; so why grieve for them?

29

as a miracle, some see *it*; and others say it is marvellous and others learn that it is ineffable; and some, after having learnt,* still do not know it.

30

this eternal spirit is unkillable, in every body, bhaarata;
so, you must not grieve for any of the living.

---

*one who knows, has studied, the veda; knowing the scriptures.

31

svadharmam api cā 'vekṣya
na vikampitum arhasi
dharmyād dhi yuddhāc chreyo 'nyat
kṣatriyasya na vidyate

32

yadṛcchayā co 'papannaṁ
svargadvāram apāvṛtam
sukhinaḥ kṣatriyāḥ pārtha
labhante yuddham īdṛśam

33

atha cet tvam imaṁ dharmyaṁ
saṁgrāmaṁ na kariṣyasi
tataḥ svadharmaṁ kīrtiṁ ca
hitvā pāpam avāpsyasi

34

akīrtiṁ cā 'pi bhūtāni
kathayiṣyanti te 'vyayām
saṁbhāvitasya cā 'kīrtir
maraṇād atiricyate

35

bhayād raṇād uparataṁ
maṁsyante tvāṁ mahārathāḥ
yeṣāṁ ca tvaṁ bahumato
bhūtvā yāsyasi lāghavam

31

and also, looking at your svadharma* you must not falter;
for, there is nothing higher for a kshatriya than a war for truth.

32

fortuitous and just, an open portal to heaven—
joyful are kshatriyas, partha, who find such a war!

33

but if you do not fight this battle of dharma,
then, forsaking your svadharma and your fame,
you will find sin.

34

besides, of your ignominy all men will tell forever,
and for the honoured infamy is worse than death.

35

that out of fear you quit the battle these maharathas will think;
and in those that once held you in great esteem, you will find contempt.

---

*inherent caste duty, here as a kshatriya warrior.

36

avācyavādāṁś ca bahūn
vadiṣyanti tavā 'hitāḥ
nindantas tava sāmarthyaṁ
tato duḥkhataraṁ nu kim

37

hato vā prāpsyasi svargaṁ
jitvā vā bhokṣyase mahīm
tasmād uttiṣṭha kaunteya
yuddhāya kṛtaniścayaḥ

38

sukhaduḥkhe same kṛtvā
lābhālābhau jayājayau
tato yuddhāya yujyasva
nai 'vaṁ pāpam avāpsyasi

39

eṣā te 'bhihitā sāṁkhye
buddhir yoge tu imāṁ śṛṇu
buddhyā yukto yayā pārtha
karmabandhaṁ prahāsyasi

40

ne 'ha 'bhikramanāśo 'sti
pratyavāyo na vidyate
svalpam apy asya dharmasya
trāyate mahato bhayāt

36

and your enemies will malign you with vile slander,
scoffing at your prowess; what can be more painful than that?

37

either being killed you will attain heaven, or, victorious, enjoy the earth;
so arise, kaunteya, resolved to fight!

38

pleasure and pain equally treat: gain, loss: victory, defeat;
then join battle—you will no sin incur.

39

i have told you about samkhya;* to the yoga of mind now listen;
yoke† your intellect with this, partha, the bonds of karma put to sword.

40

in battle, with this,** there is no-one killed, no sin to consider;
even the least bit of this dharma preserves from great fear.

---

*system of philosophy founded by kapila muni.
†yoga means to yoke; control, restrain, here.
**yoga of knowledge.

41

vyavasāyātmikā buddhir
eke 'ha kurunandana
bahuśakhā hy anantāś ca
buddhayo 'vyavasāyinām

42

yām imāṁ puṣpitāṁ vācaṁ
pravadanty avipaścitaḥ
vedavādaratāḥ pārtha
nā 'nyad astī 'ti vādinaḥ

43

kāmātmānaḥ svargaparā
janmakarmaphalapradāṃ
kriyāviśeṣabahulāṁ
bhogaiśvaryagatiṁ prati

44

bhogaiśvaryaprasaktānāṁ
tayā 'pahṛtacetasām
vyavasāyātmikā buddhiḥ
samādhau na vidhīyate

45

traiguṇyaviṣayā vedā
nistraiguṇyo bhavā 'rjuna
nirdvandvo nityasattvastho
niryogakṣema ātmavān

41

in the resolute soul, the mind is one, joy of the kurus;
many-branched and unending are the thoughts of the irresolute.

42

with these memorised flowery words those of small vision eulogise the panegyrics of the veda, partha, saying nothing else† exists.

43

their hearts of desire, svarga their ideal, the rewards of births and rites they seek;
frequent, unvarying rituals, to have pleasure and power, they perform.

44

to pleasure and power attached, their thoughts beguiled by these;
with devoted mind to attain samadhi* they do not strive.

45

with matters of the three gunas†† the vedas deal; be without the three gunas, arjuna:
free from duality; always established in sattva,‡ unattached, serene.

---

†higher.
*communion with god, liberation.
††sattva, rajas and tamas.
‡the pure guna.

46

yāvān artha udapāne
sarvataḥ saṁplutodake
tāvān sarveṣu vedeṣu
brāhmaṇasya vijānataḥ

47

karmaṇy evā 'dhikāras te
mā phaleṣu kadācana
mā karmaphalahetur bhūr
mā te saṅgo 'stv akarmaṇi

48

yogasthaḥ kuru karmāṇi
saṅgaṁ tyaktvā dhanaṁjaya
siddhyasiddhyoḥ samo bhūtvā
samatvaṁ yoga ucyate

49

dūreṇa hy avaraṁ karma
buddhiyogād dhanaṁjaya
buddhau śaraṇam anviccha
kṛpaṇāḥ phalahetavaḥ

50

buddhiyukto jahātī 'ha
ubhe sukṛtaduṣkṛte
tasmād yogāva yujyasva
yogaḥ karmasu kauśalam

46

as much use as in a well to a deluge of water everywhere:
so much in all the vedas to a brahmana of enlightenment.

47

you surely have the right to do your karma,* not to its fruit, at any time;
the fruit of karma should not become your motive, nor be attached to sloth.

48

steadfast in yoga, do your duty, renouncing attachment, dhananjaya;
success and failure becoming the same: that equanimity is called yoga.

49

far inferior is ritual to the yoked mind, dhananjaya;
in wisdom seek refuge: pitiful are those driven by gain.

50

mind yoked, you can be free here** of both good and evil;
so, to yoga devote yourself; yoga is genius at karma.

---

*natural duty.
**in this world.

51

karmajaṁ buddhiyuktā hi
phalaṁ tyaktvā manīṣiṇaḥ
janmabandhavinirmuktāḥ
padaṁ gacchanty anāmayam

52

yadā te mohakalilaṁ
buddhir vyatitariṣyati
tadā gantāsi nirvedaṁ
śrotavyasya śrutasya ca

53

śrutivipratipannā te
yadā sthāsyati niścalā
samādhāv acalā buddhis
tadā yogam avāpsyasi

54

arjuna uvāca
sthitaprajñasya kā bhāṣā
samādhisthasya keśava
sthitadhīḥ kiṁ prabhāṣeta
kim āsīta vrajeta kim

55

śrībhagavān uvāca
prajahāti yadā kāmān
sarvān pārtha manogatān
ātmany evā 'tmanā tuṣṭaḥ
sthitaprajñas tado 'cyate

51

performing karma, mind devoted, but its fruit
renouncing, wise men,
from the bondage of birth entirely freed,† come to the
place of no sickness.

52

when beyond this chaos of illusions your mind passes,
then you will arrive at indifference to what you have
heard and what you will hear.*

53

by the srutis confused:†† when your mind becomes still,
unmoving
in samadhi permanently, then you will find yoga.

54

arjuna said:
how can you tell a man of resolution, who is founded in
samadhi, kesava?‡
how does a realised one speak? how does he sit, how
walk?

55

the gracious lord said: when a man abandons all desires,
partha, which spring in the mind,
and gratifies himself in just his soul, a man of
unshakeable wisdom he is said to be.

---

†repeated birth, death and rebirth.

*srotasi refers to what you will hear in the vedas, too.

††now confused.

‡krishna.

56

duḥkheṣu anudvignamanāḥ
sukheṣu vigataspṛhaḥ
vītarāgabhayakrodhaḥ
sthitadhīr munir uncyate

57

yaḥ sarvatrā 'nabhisnehas
tat-tat prāpya śubhāśubham
nā 'bhinandati na dveṣṭi
tasya prajñā pratiṣṭhitā

58

yadā saṁharate cā 'yaṁ
kūrmo 'ṅgānī 'va sarvaśaḥ
indriyānī 'ndriyārthebhyas
tasya prajñā pratiṣṭhitā

59

viṣayā vinivartante
nirāhārasya dehinaḥ
rasavarjaṁ raso 'py asya
paraṁ dṛṣṭvā nivartate

60

yatato hy api kaunteya
puruṣasya vipaścitaḥ
indriyāṇi pramāthīni
haranti prasabhaṁ manaḥ

56

unaffected by adversity, whose mind, in fortune unmoved to desire;
free of passion, fear and anger, a true muni is called.

57

who everywhere is without affection; who, upon finding fortune or misfortune,
neither exults nor feels aversion, his wisdom is founded.

58

and when, as a tortoise completely retracts all its limbs, a man
does his senses from their objects of desire, his wisdom is founded.

59

through restraint the embodied can refrain from indulging the senses,
but not from desire; even his desires disappear at the vision of *god.*

60

of even, son of kunti, a restrained man,
his turbid senses forcibly ravish his mind.

61

tāni sarvāni saṁyamya
yukta āsīta matparah
vaśe hi yasye 'ndriyāṇi
tasya prajñā pratiṣṭhitā

62

dhyāyato viṣayān puṁsaḥ
saṅgas teṣū pajāyate
saṅgāt saṁjāyate kāmaḥ
kāmāt krodho 'bhijāyate

63

krodhād bhavati saṁmohaḥ
saṁmohāt smṛtivibhramaḥ
smṛtibhraṁśād buddhināśo
buddhināśāt praṇaśyati

64

rāgadveṣaviyuktais tu
viṣayān indriyaiś caran
ātmavaśyair vidheyātmā
prasādam adhigacchati

65

prasāde sarvaduḥkhānāṁ
hānir asyo 'pajāyate
prasannacetaso hy āśu
buddhiḥ paryavatiṣṭhate

61

all the senses restraining, the sage sits intent on me;
for, one whose senses are tamed, his wisdom is established.

62

dwelling on the objects of desire,* a man becomes attached to these;
from attachment is born desire; from desire anger arises;

63

from rage comes upheaval;† from turmoil, the wavering memory;
after the loss of memory, destruction of the mind; when the mind is destroyed, he dies.

64

emancipated from attraction and revulsion, but going among the objects of the senses,
tamed by the atman, ruled by the soul, he attains grace.

65

with grace, of all suffering the end comes;
the tranquil one's wisdom, surely, is quickly constant.

---

*sense objects; objects of sensuality.

†'delusion' is the most common translation for sammohah.

66

nā sti buddhir ayuktasya
na cā 'yuktasya bhāvanā
na cā 'bhāvayataḥ śāntir
aśāntasya kutaḥ sukham

67

indriyāṇāṁ hi caratāni
yan mano 'nuvidhīyate
tad asya harati prajñāṁ
vāyur nāvam ivā 'mbhasi

68

tasmād yasya mahābāho
nigṛhītāni sarvaśaḥ
indriyāṇi 'ndriyārthebhyas
tasya prajñā pratiṣṭhitā

69

yā niśā sarvabhūtānāṁ
tasyāṁ jāgarti saṁyamī
yasyāṁ jāgrati bhūtāni
sā niśā paśyato muneḥ

70

āpūryamāṇam acalapratiṣṭhaṁ
samudram āpaḥ praviśanti yadvat
tadvat kāmā yaṁ praviśanti sarve
sa śāntim āpnoti na kāmakāmī

66
no wisdom for the wilful, and not for the reckless faith;
and for the faithless, there is no peace; for the
peaceless, from where joy?

67
whichever of the ever-roving senses the mind yields to,
that bears his wisdom away, as the wind a boat on the
sea.

68
so, he, mahabaho, who withdraws completely
the senses from the objects of sensuality, his wisdom is
profound.

69
when night comes for all creatures, is when the ascetic
awakes;
what is waking for the rest, that is night for the
visionary.

70
always still, the ocean, though being filled by water
entering into it;
equally, he who contains all desires entering him,
acquires peace, not he who submits to desire.

71

vihāya kāmān yaḥ sarvān
pumāṁś carati niḥspṛhaḥ
nirmamo nirahaṁkāraḥ
sa śāntim adhigacchati

72

eśā brāhmī sthitiḥ pārtha
nai 'nāṁ prāpya vimuhyati
sthitvā 'syām antakāle 'pi
brahmanirvāṇam ṛcchati

71

leaving the things of desire, who roams the earth,
unattached,
without 'mine', without 'i', he attains peace.

72

this is the braahmi state,* partha; attaining to this, he is
no more tempted;
abiding in this at his final hour, as well, he goes to
brahmanirvana.†

this is the second canto of the srimad bhagavad gita named samkhya yoga

---

*union with brahman.

†nirvana: absorption; eternal bliss; highest felicity; union; dissolution in; extinction; death; vanishment.

canto 3

the yoga of action

1

arjuna uvāca
jyāyasī cet karmaṇas te
matā buddhir janārdana
tat kiṁ karmaṇi ghore māṁ
niyojayasi keśava

2

vyāmiśreṇe 'va vākyena
buddhiṁ mohayasī 'va me
tad ekaṁ vada miścitya
yena śreyo 'ham āpnuyām

3

śrībhagavān uvāca
loke 'smin dvividhā niṣṭhā
purā proktā mayā 'nagha
jñanayogena sāṁkhyānāṁ
karmayogena yogināṁ

4

na karmaṇām anārambhān
naiṣkarmyaṁ puruṣo 'śnute
na ca saṁnyasanād eva
siddhiṁ samadhigacchati

5

na hi kaścit kṣaṇam api
jātu tiṣṭhaty akarmakṛt
kāryate hy avaśah karma
sarvaḥ prakṛtijair guṇaiḥ

1

arjuna said:
if you think knowledge superior to action, janardana,
then why to this ghastly deed do you commit me,
kesava?

2

with your seemingly ambiguous words, you only confuse
my mind;
say one thing, decidedly, by which i can attain felicity.

3

the gracious lord said:
in this world, two kinds of devotion were of old ordained
by me, o sinless—
the yoga of knowledge for samkhyas, the way of deeds
for yogis.

4

by not doing his duty a man does not achieve freedom
from karma;
nor by mere abstention is transcendent perfection
attained.

5

nor, certainly, can anyone even momentarily ever stay
inactive;
because all are helplessly made to act by the prakriti-
born gunas.

6

karmendriyāṇi saṁyamya
ya āste manasā smaran
indriyārthān vimūḍhātmā
mithyācāraḥ sa ucyate

7

yas tv indriyāṇi manasā
niyamyā 'rabhate 'rjuṇa
karmendriyaiḥ karmayogam
asaktaḥ sa viśiṣyate

8

niyataṁ kuru karma tvaṁ
karma jyāyo hy akarmaṇaḥ
śarīrayātrā 'pi ca te
na prasidhyed akarmaṇaḥ

9

yajñārthāt karmaṇo 'nyatra
loko 'yam karmabandhanaḥ
tadarthaṁ karma kaunteya
muktasaṅgaḥ samācara

10

sahayajñāḥ prajāḥ sṛṣṭvā
puro 'vāca prajāpatiḥ
anena prasavisyadhvam
eṣa vo 'stu iṣṭakāmadhuk

6

he that restrains the organs of karma but continues to dwell in his mind
on the objects of sensuality, that foolish soul is deemed a hypocrite.

7

but, he who, restraining the senses with the mind, arjuna, engages
the organs of action in karma yoga, dispassionately—he excels.

8

you must always do your duty; because action is higher than inactivity;
besides, you will not succeed even in keeping your body through inertia.

9

all karma other than that done as an offering binds this world in rebirth;
for that, act, kaunteya, free from attachment, consummately.

10

together with sacrifice creating men, of old prajapati* said,
'by this, you will generate and multiply; let this be the yielder of your wishes.

*brahma, the creator; lord of the people.

11

devān bhāvayatā 'nena
te devā bhāvayantu vaḥ
parasparaṁ bhāvayantaḥ
śreyaḥ param avāpsyatha

12

iṣṭān bhogān hi vo devā
dāsyante yajñabhāvitāh
tair dattān apradāyai 'bhyo
yo bhuṅkte stena eva saḥ

13

yajñaśiṣṭāśinaḥ santo
mucyante sarvakilbiṣaiḥ
bhuñjate te tv aghaṁ pāpā
ye pacanty ātmakāraṇāt

14

annād bhavanti bhūtāni
parjanyād annasaṁbhavaḥ
yajñād bhavati parjanyo
yajñaḥ karmasamudbhavaḥ

15

karma brahmodbhavaṁ viddhi
brahmā 'kṣarasamudbhavam
tasmāt sarvagataṁ brahma
nityaṁ yajñe pratiṣṭhitam

11

'adore the devas by this; let the devas succour you;
by each other nourished, supreme felicity you will have.

12

'bound by the nurture of sacrifice, the gods will surely give you the pleasures you desire;
one who enjoys these gifts, without giving to them, he is certainly a thief.'

13

the saintly who eat the leftovers of a sacrifice are liberated from all sins;
but the sinful eat sin, who cook food just for themselves.

14

from food are born beings; from rain, food grows;
from sacrifice, come the rains; sacrifice from karma* springs.

15

karma from brahma arises, know; brahma of the imperishable is born;
so, ubiquitous brahma always abides in sacrifice.

---

*action, duty, caste duty, sacred duty.

16

evaṁ pravartitaṁ cakraṁ
nā 'nuvartayatī 'ha yaḥ
aghāyur indriyārāmo
moghaṁ pārtha sa jīvati

17

yas tu ātmaratir eva syād
ātmatṛptaś ca mānavaḥ
ātmany eva ca samtuṣṭas
tasya kāryaṁ na vidyate

18

nai 'va tasya kṛtenā 'rtho
nā 'krtene 'ha kaścana
na cā sya sarvabhūteṣu
kaścid arthavyapāśrayaḥ

19

tasmād asaktaḥ satataṁ
kāryaṁ karma samācara
asakto hy ācaran karma
param āpnoti pūruṣaḥ

20

karmaṇai 'va hi saṁsiddhim
āsthitā janakādayaḥ
lokasaṁgraham evā 'pi
saṁpaśyan kartum arhasi

16

hence, this turning wheel, who does not live by it here,
lives in sin, indulging the senses—in vain, partha, he
lives.

17

but for him who is devoted only to the atman,* and
remains absorbed in the atman, the man
who, also, is fulfilled only in the soul—for him no duty
is ordained.

18

he surely has nothing to gain here, either by doing or
by not doing;
nor does he, among all the living, seek any gain.

19

thus, without attachment, always do your duty
impeccably;
for, by performing karma without attachment man
attains the supreme.

20

indeed, only through karma did in absolute perfection
abide janaka** and others;
besides, also considering the good of the world, you
must act.

---

*soul; self.

**the rajarishi, king janaka, sita's father, rama's father-in-law.

21

yad-yad ācarati śreṣṭhas
tad-tad eve 'taro janaḥ
sa yat pramāṇaṁ kurute
lokas tad anuvartate

22

na me pārthā 'sti kartavyaṁ
triṣu lokeṣu kiṁcana
nā 'navāptam avāptavyaṁ
varta eva ca karmaṇi

23

yadi hy ahaṁ na varteyaṁ
jātu karmaṇy atandritaḥ
mama vartmā 'nuvartante
manuṣyāḥ pārtha sarvaśaḥ

24

utsīdeyur ime lokā
na kuryāṁ karma ced aham
saṁkarasya ca kartā syām
upahanyām imāḥ prajāḥ

25

saktāḥ karmany avidvāṁso
yathā kurvanti bhārata
kuryād vidvāṃs tahā 'saktaś
cikīrṣur lokasaṁgraham

21

whatever a great man does: all that other men also do;
whatever norm he sets, that all the world follows.

22

not for me, partha, is there any duty in the three worlds,
nor anything to attain that is unattained; and i am always at work.

23

surely, if ever i am not at my work, tirelessly,
my path would be followed by men, partha, of every walk.

24

plunged into ruin these worlds, if i did not do my work;
and i would be the cause of crossbreeding,* diminishing these generations.

25

as the ignorant perform karma with desire, attachment, bhaarata,
so must the knowing act, unattached, wanting the weal of the world.

---

*varnasamkarasya: anarchy through mixing of the castes.

26

na buddhibhedaṁ janayed
ajñānāṁ karmasaṅginām
joṣayet sarvakarmāṇi
vidvān yuktaḥ samācaran

27

prakṛteḥ kriyamāṇāni
guṇaiḥ karmāṇi sarvaśaḥ
ahaṁkāravimūḍhātmā
kartā 'ham iti manyate

28

tattvavit tu mahābāho
guṇakarmavibhāgayoḥ
guṇā guṇeṣu vartanta
iti matvā na sajjate

29

prakṛter guṇasaṁmūḍhāḥ
sajjante guṇakarmasu
tān akṛtsnavido mandān
kṛtsnavin na vicālayet

30

mayi sarvāṇi karmāṇi
saṁnyasyā 'dhyātmacetasā
nirāśīr nirmamo bhūtvā
yudhyasva vigatajvaraḥ

26

not creating confusion in the minds of the unknowing attached to karma,
silently the wise man does all his work, yoked, absorbed.

27

nature's essences perform karma, in every way;
he who is beguiled by egotism thinks, 'i am the doer'.

28

but he who knows the truth, mahabaho, about the difference between guna and karma—
the gunas act upon the gunas—so knowing, is not attached.

29

those deluded by the gunas of nature become enmeshed in karma born of the gunas;
those dull ones that do not know the *all*,* a knower of everything must not agitate.

30

to me all karma consigning, to the atman your thought;
becoming desireless, dispassionate, do battle, leaving panic.

*the truth, brahman.

31

ye me matam idaṁ nityam
anutiṣṭhanti mānavāḥ
śraddhāvanto 'nasūyanto
mucyante te 'pi karmabhiḥ

32

ye tv etad abhyasūyanto
nā 'nutiṣṭhanti me matam
sarvajñānavimūḍhāṁs tān
viddhi naṣṭān acetasaḥ

33

sadṛśaṁ ceṣṭate svasyāḥ
prakṛter jñānavān api
prakṛtiṁ yānti bhūtāni
nigrahaḥ kiṁ kariṣyati

34

indriyasye 'ndriyasyā 'rthe
rāgadveṣau vyavasthitau
tayor na vaśam āgacchet
tau hy asya paripanthinau

35

śreyān svadharmo viguṇaḥ
paradharmāt svanuṣṭhitāt
svadharme nidhanaṁ śreyaḥ
paradharmo bhayāvahaḥ

31

this my teaching, those men who always follow,
with faith, without derision, are also liberated from karma.

32

but they who slight this, do not follow my precept,
fools to all knowledge, are, know, lost, insensate.

33

in concord with his nature, acts even the wise man;
nature, beings obey—what can inhibition achieve?

34

for the senses, attraction and revulsion towards the objects of sensuality are inexorable;
no man must come under their sway, for they are his enemies.

35

better in one's own dharma, flawed, than another's dharma immaculately done;
death in one's own dharma is auspicious; another's dharma is dangerous.

36

arjuna uvāca

atha kena prayukto 'yaṁ
pāpaṁ carati pūruṣaḥ
anicchann api vārṣṇeya
balād iva niyojitaḥ

37

śrībhagavān uvāca

kāma eṣa krodha eṣa
rajoguṇasamudbhavaḥ
mahāśano mahāpāpmā
viddhy enam iha vairiṇam

38

dhūmenā 'vriyate vahnir
yathā 'darśo malena ca
yatho 'lbenā 'vrto garbhas
tathā tense 'dam āvṛtam

39

āvṛtaṁ jñānam etena
jñānino nityavairiṇā
kāmarūpeṇa kaunteya
anṣpūreṇā 'nalena ca

40

indriyāṇi mano buddhir
asyā 'dhiṣṭhānam ucyate
etair vimohayaty eṣa
jñānam āvṛtya dehinam

36

arjuna said:
then what makes a man to commit sin,
even unwillingly, vaarshaneya, with force as if coerced?

37

the gracious lord said:
it is desire, it is anger, arisen from the rajoguna*—
voracious, direly sinful, know this, here, for an enemy.

38

as fire is obscured by smoke and a mirror by dust,
as the womb hides an embryo, so is *it* hidden by that.

39

shrouded, wisdom by this, of the wise, the constant enemy,
with lust's form, kaunteya, and an insatiable fire.

40

senses, mind, intellect, its abode, it's said;
by these confounding, it shrouds the wisdom of the embodied.

---

*the second guna, mode of prakriti, of the essence of passion.

41

tasmāt tvam indriyāṇy ādau
niyamya bharatarṣabha
pāpmānaṁ prajahi hy enaṁ
jñānavijñānanāśanam

42

indriyāṇi parāṇy āhur
indriyebhyaḥ paraṁ manaḥ
manasas tu parā buddhir
yo buddheḥ paratas tu saḥ

43

evaṁ buddheḥ paraṁ buddhvā
saṁstabhyā 'tmānam ātmanā
jahi śatruṁ mahābāho
kāmarūpaṁ durāsadam

41

so, your senses first control, bharatarishabha;
kill this malignant thing, for this is the ruiner of knowledge and wisdom.

42

the senses are lofty, they say; higher than the senses is mind;
and beyond mind is intellect; but past intellect is *he.*

43

so, knowing what is beyond the intellect, stilling the self with the soul,
vanquish, mahabaho, the enemy, lust-formed, unassailable.

this is the third canto of the srimad bhagavad gita named karma yoga

canto 4

the way of knowledge

1

śrībhagavān uvāca
imaṁ vivasvate yogaṁ
proktavān aham avyayam
vivasvān manave prāha
manur ikṣvākave 'bravit

2

evaṁ paramparāprāptam
imaṁ rājarṣayo viduḥ
sa kālene 'ha mahatā
yogo naṣṭaḥ paraṁtapa

3

sa evā 'yaṁ mayā te 'dya
yogaḥ proktaḥ purātanaḥ
bhakto 'si me sakhā ce 'ti
rahasyaṁ hy etad uttamam

4

arjuna uvāca
aparaṁ bhavato janma
paraṁ janma vivasvataḥ
katham etad vijānīyāṁ
tvam ādau proktavān iti

5

bahūni me vyatītani
janmāni tava cā .rjuna
tāny ahaṁ veda sarvāṇi
na tvaṁ vettha paraṁtapa

1

the gracious lord said:
this yoga to vivaswat[*] i revealed, immortal;
vivaswat to manu[†] taught it; manu to ikshavaku[‡]
imparted it.

2

so, by lineal tradition received, this the rajarishis[**] knew;
after great time, here, the yoga was lost, parantapa.

3

that very same have i to you today revealed, the ancient
yoga:
for you are my devotee and my friend, because this is
the secret supreme.

4

arjuna said:
recent your birth, earlier the birth of vivaswat;
so how do i comprehend this—you first taught him?

5

myriad births of mine are past, and yours, arjuna;
these i know, every one; you do not know, parantapa.

---

[*]the sun god; surya deva.
[†]surya's son vaivaswata manu: progenitor of the manushyas or manavas, humankind.
[‡]manu's son, great king, founder of the suryavamsa, royal house of the sun, into which rama was born.
[**]royal sages, saintly kings.

6

ajo 'pi sann avyayātmā
bhūtānām īśvaro 'pi san
prakṛtiṁ svām adhiṣṭhāya
saṁbhavāmy ātmamāyayā

7

yadā-yadā hi dharmasya
glānir bhavati bhārata
abhyutthānam adharmasya
tadā 'tmānaṁ sṛjāmy aham

8

paritrāṇāya sādhūnāṁ
vināśāya ca duṣkṛtām
dharmasaṁsthāpanārthāya
saṁbhavāmi yuge-yuge

9

janma karma ca me divyam
evaṁ yo vetti tattvataḥ
tyaktvā dehaṁ punarjanma
nai 'ti mām eti so 'rjuna

10

vītarāgabhayakrodhā
manmayā mām upāśritāḥ
bahavo jñānatapasā
pūtā madbhāvam āgatāḥ

6

though un-born, my soul immortal, the lord of creatures though being,
abiding in my own nature, i incarnate through my soul's maya.*

7

whenever there is a decline of dharma, bhaarata,
an ascendancy of adharma, then myself i manifest.

8

for the deliverance of the good and for the destruction of sinners;
in order to establish dharma, i come from age to age.

9

so, who my divine birth and deeds knows truly,
after leaving the body does not find rebirth; he finds me, arjuna.

10

gone, passion, fear, anger; absorbed in me, sheltering in me,
many, purified by wisdom's penance, have come to my being.

---

*mysterious power of illusion.

11

ye yathā maṁ prapadyante
tāṁs tathai 'va bhajāmy aham
mama vartmā 'nuvartante
manuṣyāḥ pārtha sarvaśaḥ

12

kāṅkṣantaḥ karmaṇāṁ siddhiṁ
yajanta iha devatāḥ
kṣipraṁ hi mānuṣe loke
siddhir bhavati karmajā

13

cāturvarṇyaṁ mayā sṛṣṭaṁ
guṇakarmavibhāgaśaḥ
tasya kartāram api māṁ
viddhy akartāram avyayam

14

na māṁ karmāṇi limpanti
na me karmaphale spṛhā
iti māṁ yo 'bhijānāti
karmabhir na sa badhyate

15

evaṁ jñātvā kṛtaṁ karma
pūrvair api mumukṣubhiḥ
kuru karmai 'va tasmāt tvaṁ
pūrvaiḥ purvataraṁ kṛtam

11

as they come to me, so do i cherish them;
my path men walk, partha, on every path.

12

those who wish for gain from karma sacrifice here to the gods;
for, speedily in the world of men gain attends on ritual.

13

the four varnas, my creation: by gunas, karma, divided;
its creator, also, know that i am actless, immutable.

14

i am not by karma tainted; i do not desire the fruit of karma;
one who recognises me to be thus, he is not bound to karma.

15

this knowing, the ancients, too, performed karma, the seekers after mukti;*
so must you do your duty, as the ancients did of old.

---

*liberation; final salvation.

16

kiṁ karma kim akarme 'ti
kavayo 'py atra mohitāh
tat te karma pravakṣyāmi
yaj jñātvā mokṣyase 'śubhāt

17

karmaṇo hy api boddhavyaṁ
boddhavyaṁ ca vikarmaṇaḥ
akarmaṇaś ca boddhavyaṁ
gahanā karmaṇo gatiḥ

18

karmaṇy akarma yaḥ paśyed
akarmaṇi ca karma yaḥ
sa buddhimān manuṣyeṣu
sa yuktaḥ kṛtsnakarmakṛt

19

yasya sarve samārambhāḥ
kāmasaṁkalpavarjitāh
jñanāgnidagdhakarmānaṁ
tam āhuḥ paṇḍitaṁ budhāḥ

20

tyaktvā karmaphalāsaṅgaṁ
nityatṛpto nirāśrayaḥ
karmaṇy abhipravṛtto 'pi
nani 'va kiṁcit karoti sah

16

what is karma, what is akarma? by this even the seers are baffled;
of that karma i will tell you, knowing which you will be saved from every ill.

17

what karma is must also be understood, and what is forbidden karma;
and what is not karma be known—deep is the way of karma.

18

who in work repose sees, and in inactivity ado,
he is wise among men; he is a sage, all his duty done.

19

whose every endeavour is without desire's intent;
whose deeds are burnt in wisdom's fire, him the wise call a sage.

20

renouncing attachment for the fruit of work, always contented, independent,
though incessantly at work, he does nothing at all.

21

nirāśīr yatacittātmā
tyaktasarvaparigrahaḥ
śārīraṁ kevalaṁ karma
kurvan nā 'pnoti kilbiṣam

22

yadṛcchālābhasaṁtuṣṭo
dvandvātīto vimatsaraḥ
samaḥ siddhāv asiddhau ca
kṛtvā 'pi na nibadhyate

23

gatasaṅgasya muktasya
jñānāvasthitacetasaḥ
yajñāyā 'carataḥ karma
samagraṁ pravilīyate

24

brahmā 'rpaṇaṁ brahma havir
brahmāgnau brahmaṇā hutam
brahmai 'va tena gantavyaṁ
brahmakarmasamādhinā

25

daivam evā 'pare yajñaṁ
yoginaḥ paryupāsate
brahmāgnāv apare yajñaṁ
yajñenai 'vo 'pajuhvati

21

desireless, he of restrained mind, leaving all possessions,
just the body doing work, finds no sin.

22

with whatever chance gives contented, beyond duality,
without envy,
and equable in success, failure—though doing, he is not
bound.

23

whose attachments are gone, who is free, mind founded
in wisdom;
who acts only as a sacrifice—all his karma dissolves
entirely.

24

brahman the sacrifice, brahman the oblation; brahman
the fire into which brahman makes the offering;
brahman he surely attains through the devotion of
brahmakarma.*

25

only with sacrifices to the devas, some yogis worship;
into the fire of brahman others sacrifice itself as sacrifice
offer.

---

*working for brahman; serving brahman.

26

śrotrādīnī 'ndriyāṇy anye
saṁyamāgniṣu juhvati
śabdādīn viṣayān anya
indriyāgniṣu juhvati

27

sarvāṇī 'ndriyakarmāṇi
prāṇakarmāṇi cā 'pare
ātmasaṁyamayogāgnau
juhvati jñānadīpite

28

dravyayajñās tapoyajñā
yogayajñās tathā 'pare
svādhyāyajñānayajñāś ca
yatayaḥ saṁśitavratāḥ

29

apāne juhvati prāṇaṁ
prāṇe 'pānaṁ tathā 'pare
prāṇāpānagatī ruddhvā
prāṇāyāmaparāyaṇāḥ

30

apare niyatāhārāḥ
prāṇān prāṇeṣu juhvati
sarve 'py ete yajñavido
yajñakṣapitakalmaṣāḥ

26

hearing, the other senses, some into restraint's fire offer;
sound, the other objects of sensuality, others into the fire of the senses offer.

27

all the senses' karma and the karma of life, others
offer into self-restraint's yogic fire, kindled by wisdom.

28

material sacrifice; penance as sacrifice; with yoga, too, others sacrifice;
sacred study and knowledge, sacrifice the ascetics of stern vows.

29

inhaling they offer into exhalation; exhaling into in-breath, as well, others:
prana, apana's,* movement stilling, those devoted to pranayama.

30

others curb what they eat, into prana, prana offer;
all these, also, knowers of sacrifice: by sacrifice, their sins expelled.

*inward and outward breaths.

31

yajñaśiṣṭāmṛtabhujo
yānti brahma sanātanam
nā 'yaṁ loko 'sty ayajñasya
kuto 'nyaḥ kurusattama

32

evaṁ bahuvidhā yajñā
vitatā brahmaṇo mukhe
karmajān viddhi tān sarvān
evaṁ jñātvā vimokṣyase

33

śreyān dravyamayād yajñāj
jñānayajñaḥ paraṁtapa
sarvaṁ karmā 'khilaṁ pārtha
jñāne parisamāpyate

34

tad viddhi praṇipātena
paripraśnema sevayā
upadekṣyanti te jñānaṁ
jñāninas tattvadarśinaḥ

35

yaj jñātvā na punar moham
evaṁ yāsyasi pāṇḍava
yena bhūtāny aśeṣeṇa
drakṣyasy ātmany atho mayi

31

eating sacrificial remains, ambrosia, they go to eternal brahman;
not this world is for the unsacrificing, much less any other, best of kurus.

32

so, many kinds of sacrifice are spread across brahman's face;
karma-born, know, all these; so knowing, you will become free.

33

better than sacrifice of wealth, the devotion of wisdom, parantapa;
all karma, in entirety, partha, culminates in wisdom.

34

that learn, through homage, by inquiry and service:
the wise, seers of truth, will teach you wisdom.

35

which knowing, not again will delusion so torment you, pandava;
with this, all creatures, without exception, you will see in yourself, and in me.

36

api ced asi pāpebhyaḥ
sarvebhyaḥ pāpakṛttamaḥ
sarvaṁ jñānaplavenai 'va
vṛjinaṁ saṁtariṣyasi

37

yathai 'dhāṁsi samiddho 'gnir
bhasmasāt kurute 'rjuna
jñānāgniḥ sarvakarmāṇi
bhasmasāt kurute tathā

38

na hi jñānena sadṛśaṁ
pavitram iha vidyate
tat svayaṁ yogasaṁsiddhaḥ
kālenā 'tmani vindati

39

śraddhāvāṁl labhate jñānaṁ
tatparaḥ saṁyatendriyaḥ
jñānaṁ labdhvā parām śāntim
acireṇā 'dhigacchati

40

ajñaś cā 'śraddahānaś ca
saṁśayātmā vinaśyati
nā 'yaṁ loko 'sti na paro
nā sukhaṁ saṁśayātmanaḥ

36
even if you, of sinners, of them all, are the greatest sinner,
all distress, by wisdom's boat, you will surely cross.

37
just as its fuel of wood a fire makes ashes, arjuna,
wisdom's fire all karma to ashes turns, as surely.

38
nothing to equal wisdom in purity exists here;
that, of himself, one evolved in yoga, in time, within himself attains.

39
he of faith attains wisdom: absorbed, senses restrained;
wisdom gained, to supreme peace, also, he quickly comes.

40
the ignorant and faithless and the doubting soul perishes;
not this world, not the next, nor happiness for the doubting soul.

41

yogasaṁnyastakarmāṇaṁ
jñānasaṁchinnasaṁśayam
ātmavantaṁ na karmāṇi
nibadhnanti dhanaṁjaya

42

tasmād ajñānasaṁbhūtaṁ
hṛtsthaṁ jñānāsinā 'tmanaḥ
chittvai 'naṁ saṁśayaṁ yogam
ātiṣṭho 'ttiṣṭha bhārata

41

through yoga renouncing karma, with wisdom severing doubt,
a self-possessed one no karma binds, dhananjaya.

42

so, cut away ignorance-born doubt seated in your heart, with wisdom's soul sword;
turn to yoga—arise, bhaarata!

this is the fourth canto of the srimad bhagavad gita named gyana yoga

canto 5

the way of renunciation

1

arjuna uvāca
saṁnyāsaṁ karmaṇāṁ kṛṣṇa
punar yogaṁ ca śaṁsasi
yac chreya etayor ekaṁ
tan me brūhi suniścitam

2

śrībhagavān uvāca
saṁnyāsaḥ karmayogaś ca
niḥśreyasakarāv ubhau
tayos tu karmasaṁnyāsāt
karmayogo viśiṣyate

3

jñeyaḥ sa nityasaṁnyāsī
yo na dveṣṭi na kāṅkṣati
nirdvandvo hi mahābāho
sukhaṁ bandhāt pramucyate

4

sāṁkhyayogau pṛthag bālāḥ
pravadanti na paṇḍitāḥ
ekam apy āsthitaḥ samyag
ubhayor vindate phalaṁ

5

yat sāṁkhyaiḥ prāpyate sthānaṁ
tad yogair api gamyate
ekaṁ sāṁkhyaṁ ca yogaṁ ca
yaḥ paśyati sa paśyati

1

arjuna said:
renunciation of karma, krishna, then again, yoga you extol;
which one of the two is better for me, say for certain.

2

the gracious lord said:
sannyasa and karma yoga effect liberation, both;
but of the two, doing karma is superior to inaction.

3

know him as a constant renunciate, who neither dislikes nor desires;
for, detached from duality, mahabaho, he is easily freed from bondage.

4

the callow say that samkhya and yoga are different, not the wise;
for, who is absorbed in one, of both enjoys the fruit.

5

the condition the samkhyas achieve, that yogis also attain;
and as one, who samkhya and yoga sees, he sees.

6

saṁnyāsas tu mahābāho
duḥkham āptum ayogataḥ
yogayukto munir brahma
nacireṇā 'dhigacchati

7

yogayukto viśuddhātmā
vijitātmā jitendriyaḥ
sarvabhūtātmabhūtātmā
kurvann api na lipyate

8

nai 'va kiṁcit karomī 'ti
yukto manyeta tattvavit
paśyañ śṛṇvan spṛśañ jighrann
aśnan gacchan svapañ śvasan

9

pralapan visṛjan gṛhṇann
unmiṣan nimiṣann api
indriyāṇī 'ndriyārtheṣu
vartanta iti dhārayan

10

brahmaṇy ādhāya karmāṇi
saṅgaṁ tyaktvā karoti yaḥ
lipyate na sa pāpena
padmapattram ivā 'mbhasā

6

but sannyasa, mighty-armed, is difficult to attain without yoga;
the sage yoked to yoga, to brahman swiftly comes.

7

who is absorbed in yoga, pure soul, master of his mind, subduer of the senses,
who is the soul of all souls—though he does, he is not tainted.

8

'i do nothing' a yukta* thinks, a knower of truth:
while seeing, hearing, touching, smelling, eating, moving, sleeping, breathing,

9

speaking, emitting, ingesting, staring and blinking:
the senses in sensuality are engaged—in this awareness.

10

resigning his karma to brahman, without attachment, who works:
he is not stained by sin, as a lotus leaf by water.

---

*a yoked one, who is united with the divine.

11

kāyena manasā buddhyā
kevalair indriyair api
yoginaḥ karma kurvanti
saṅgaṁ tyaktvā 'tmaśuddhaye

12

yuktaḥ karmaphalaṁ tyaktvā
śāntim āpnoti naiṣṭhikīm
anyuktaḥ kāmakāreṇa
phale sakto nibadhyate

13

sarvakarmāṇi manasā
saṁnyasyā 'ste sukhaṁ vaśī
navadvāre pure dehī
nai 'va kurvan na kārayan

14

na kartṛitvaṁ na karmāṇi
lokasya sṛjati prabhuḥ
na karmaphalasaṁyogaṁ
svabhāvas tu pravartate

15

nā 'datte kasyacit pāpaṁ
na cai 'va sukṛtaṁ vibhuḥ
ajñānenā 'vṛtaṁ jñānaṁ
tena muhyanti jantavaḥ

11

with the body, with the mind, with the intellect, or merely with the senses,
yogis perform karma, leaving attachment—to purify the soul.

12

the yoked, sacrificing the fruit of karma, attains profound peace;
the unyoked, moved by desire, devoted to the fruit, is bound.

13

all karma with the mind relinquishing, dwells the restrained one, at ease,
in the city of nine doors,* the embodied—surely, neither doing nor causing.†

14

neither doer nor deed for the world, the lord creates;
not union of work with its fruit; only nature acts.

15

neither anybody's sin nor, indeed, their virtue does *god* assume;
wisdom is shrouded by ignorance; by this the living are deluded.

---

*the body of nine inlets.

†anything to be done.

16

jñānena tu tad ajñānaṁ
yeṣāṁ nāśitam ātmanaḥ
teṣām ādityavaj jñānaṁ
prakāśayati tat param

17

tadbuddhayas tadātmānas
tanniṣṭhās tatparāyaṇāḥ
gacchanty apunarāvṛttiṁ
jñānanirdhūtakalmaṣāḥ

18

vidyāvinayasaṁpanne
brāhmaṇe gavi hastini
śuni cai 'va śvapāke ca
paṇḍitāḥ samadarśinaḥ

19

ihai 'va tair jitaḥ sargo
yeṣāṁ sāmye sthitaṁ manaḥ
nirdoṣaṁ hi samaṁ brahma
tasmād brahmaṇi te sthitāḥ

20

na prahṛṣyet priyaṁ prāpya
no 'dvijet prāpya cā 'priyam
sthirabuddhir asaṁmūdho
brahmavid brahmaṇi sthitaḥ

16

but whose ignorance is destroyed by knowledge of the atman,
their sunlike wisdom illumines *that,* highest.

17

that their mind, that their soul, that their faith, that their devotion—
they go to non-return, by wisdom their sins destroyed.

18

a brahmana endowed with learning, humility; a cow, an elephant,
and even a dog and a dog-eater,* the wise see as equal.

19

even here, they conquer nature, whose minds are founded in equalness;
because brahman is immaculate, equal, so they abide in brahman.

20

not elated at getting the agreeable and not dejected upon finding the unpleasant;
mind calm, undeluded, the knower of brahman in brahman dwells.

---

*chandala.

21

bāhyasparśeṣu asaktātmā
vindaty ātmani yat sukham
sa brahmayogayuktātmā
sukham akṣayam aśnute

22

ye hi saṁparśajā bhogā
duḥkhayonaya eva te
ādyantavantaḥ kaunteya
na teṣu ramate budhaḥ

23

śaknotī 'hai 'va yah soḍhuṁ
prāk śarīravimokṣaṇāt
kāmakrodhodbhavaṁ vegaṁ
sa yuktaḥ sa sukhī naraḥ

24

yo 'ntaḥsukho 'ntarārāmas
tathā 'ntarjyotir eva yaḥ
sa yogī brahmanirvāṇaṁ
brahmabhūto 'dhigacchati

25

labhante brahmanirvāṇaṁ
ṛṣayaḥ kṣīṇakalmaṣāḥ
chinnadvaidhā yatātmānaḥ
sarvabhūtahite ratāḥ

21

who is detached from the outward touch,* finds the bliss in the atman;
the one yoked in brahman through yoga, he immortal bliss enjoys.

22

surely, the pleasures of the touch of the senses, they are only wombs of sorrow;
they begin and end, kaunteya; not in them dwells a wise man.

23

who can, even here, before leaving the body, endure the lust- and anger-born rush, he is a yukta; he is the happy man.

24

who joy within, rest within, and also light only within finds;
that yogi dissolution in brahman, union with brahman, attains.

25

those rishis find brahmanirvana, whose sins are exhausted,
doubts scattered, minds restrained: to the felicity of all beings devoted.

---

*of sensual contact, pleasure.

26

kāmakrodhaviyuktānāṁ
yatīnāṁ yatacetasām
abhito brahmanirvāṇaṁ
vartate viditātmanām

27

sparśān kṛtvā bahir bāhyāṁś
cakṣuś cai 'va 'ntare bhruvoḥ
prāṇāpānau samau kṛtvā
nāsābhyantaracāriṇau

28

yatendriyamanobuddhir
munir mokṣaparāyaṇaḥ
vigatecchābhayakrodho
yaḥ sadā mukta eva saḥ

29

bhoktāraṁ yajñatapasāṁ
sarvalokamaheśvaram
suhṛdaṁ sarvabhūtānāṁ
jñātvā māṁ śāntim ṛcchati

26

freed from lust, anger, yatis, with minds restrained,
live subsumed in brahmanirvana, those who know the atman.

27

outward objects of sensuality shutting out, and gaze fixed between the brows;
making equal outward and inward breath, moving within the nose;

28

with restrained senses, mind and intellect, the sage devoted to liberation,
who has departed desire, fear and anger, he is surely always free.

29

enjoyer of sacrifices and penance, great lord of all worlds,
friend to all beings—*me*, knowing, he comes to peace.

this is the fifth canto of the srimad bhagavad gita named sannyasa yoga

canto 6

the way of meditation

1

śrībhagavān uvāca
anāśritaḥ karmaphalaṁ
kāryaṁ karma karoti yaḥ
sa saṁnyāsī ca yogī ca
na niragnir na cā 'kriyaḥ

2

yaṁ saṁnyāsam iti prāhur
yogaṁ taṁ viddhi pāṇḍava
na hy asaṁnyastasaṁkalpo
yogī bhavati kaścana

3

ārurukṣor muner yogaṁ
karma kāraṇam ucyate
yogārūḍhasya tasyai va
śamaḥ kāraṇam ucyate

4

yadā hi ne 'ndriyārtheṣu
na karmasu anuṣajjate
sarvasaṁkalpasaṁnyāsī
yogārūḍhas tado 'cyate

5

uddhared ātmanā 'tmānaṁ
nā tmānam avasādayet
ātmai 'va hy ātmano bandhur
ātmai 'va ripur ātmanaḥ

1

the gracious lord said:
not seeking karma's fruit, who does his ordained work,
he is the sannyasi and the yogi; and not one without
the fire,* and not him without ritual.

2

so, what they call sannyasa, know that is yoga, pandava;
for, without renouncing desire, no one becomes a yogi.

3

for the sage who aspires to yoga, karma is the way, it's
told;
who has attained yoga, only for him is quiescence the
way, they say.

4

only when neither to the objects of sensuality attached,
nor to action clinging,
he who renounces all desire is said to have attained
yoga.

5

raise yourself through the atman; never abase yourself;
for, only you are your own friend; you alone, your own
enemy.

6

bandhur ātmā 'tmanas tasya
yenā 'tmai 'vā 'tmanā jitaḥ
anātmanas tu śatrutve
vartetā 'tmai 'va śatruvat

7

jitātmanaḥ praśāntasya
paramātmā samāhitaḥ
śītoṣṇasukhaduḥkheṣu
tathā mānāpamānayoḥ

8

jñānavijñānatrpṭātmā
kūṭastho vijitendriyaḥ
yukta ity ucyate yogī
samaloṣṭāśmakāñncanaḥ

9

suhṛnmitrāryudāsīna-
madhyasthadveṣyabandhuṣu
sādhuṣv api ca pāpeṣu
samabuddhir viśiṣyate

10

yogī yuñjīta satatam
ātmānaṁ rahasi sthitaḥ
ekākī yatacittātmā
nirāśīr aparigrahaḥ

6

his atman is his friend only to him who has mastered himself;
for the uncontrolled, his very soul is hostile like an enemy.

7

who has conquered himself, who is tranquil, his soul is entirely composed,
in heat and cold, joy and sorrow, also, in honour and ignominy.

8

in knowledge and wisdom, fulfilled, unshakeable, master of his senses;
that yogi is said to be yoked for whom the clod of earth, a stone and gold are the same.

9

with the friend, the companion, an enemy, a stranger, an arbiter, an odious man, a relative,
as well as a saint and a sinner, he who is equal-minded, excels.

10

the yogi should constantly yoke himself: in seclusion, alone, heart and mind controlled, without desire and possession.

11

śucau deśe pratiṣṭhāpya
sthiram āsanam ātmanaḥ
nā 'tyucchritaṁ nā 'tinīcaṁ
cailājinakuśottaram

12

tatrat 'kāgraṁ manaḥ kṛtvā
yatacittendriyakriyaḥ
upaviśyā 'sane yuñjyād
yogam ātmaviśuddhaye

13

samaṁ kāyaśirogrīvaṁ
dhārayann acalaṁ sthiraḥ
saṁprekṣya nāsikāgraṁ svaṁ
diśaś cā 'navalokayan

14

praśāntātma vigatabhīr
brahamacārivrate sthitaḥ
manaḥ saṁyamya maccitto
yukta āsīta matparaḥ

15

yuñjann evaṁ sadā 'tmānaṁ
yogī niyatamānasaḥ
śāntiṁ nirvāṇaparamāṁ
matsaṁsthām adhigacchati

11

in a clean place, setting his seat firm, himself,
neither too high nor too low, with kusa grass, cloth and
deerskin, one over the other.

12

there, making his mind one-pointed, controlling his
thought and senses;
sitting upon the seat, he should absorb himself in yoga,
to purify his heart.

13

aligning body, head and neck, keeping still and steady;
fixing his gaze on the tip of his nose, and not looking
around;

14

serene, fearless, steadfast in the vow of celibacy;
mind controlled, intent on me, yoked, he sits devoted to
me.

15

thus yoking himself always, the yogi of subdued mind
to peace, supreme nirvana which abides in me, attains.

16

nā 'tyaśnatas tu yogo 'str
na cai 'kāntam anaśnataḥ
na cā 'tisvapnaśīlasya
jāgrato nai 'va cā 'rjuna

17

yuktāhāravihārasya
yuktaceṣṭasya karmasu
yuktasvapnāvabodhasya
yogo bhavati duḥkhahā

18

yadā viniyataṁ cittam
ātmany evā 'vatiṣṭhate
niḥspṛhaḥ sarvakāmebhyo
yukta ity uncyate tadā

19

yathā dīpo nivātastho
ne 'ṅgate so 'pamā smṛtā
yogino yatacittasya
yuñjato yogam ātmanaḥ

20

yatro 'paramate cittaṁ
niruddhaṁ yogasevayā
yatra cai 'vā 'tmanā 'tmānaṁ
paśyann ātmani tuṣyati

16

not for one who eats too much is yoga, nor for him who overly fasts;
and not for him given to too much sleep, nor yet for the overly wakeful, arjuna.

17

who is restrained in food and pleasure, devoted in thought and deed;
moderate in sleep and waking, attains yoga, leaving sorrow.

18

when the restrained mind is founded exclusively in the atman,
indifferent to every desire, then he is said to be a yukta.

19

as a lamp in a windless place does not flicker: similar, it is recorded,
is a yogi of restrained thought, engaged in the yoga of the atman.

20

where thought ceases, curbed by the practise of yoga;
and where, also, the mind sees the soul, and is fulfilled in the atman;

21

sukham ātyantikaṁ yat tad
buddhigrāhyam atīndriyam
vetti yatra na 'cai 'vā 'yaṁ
sthitaś calati tattvataḥ

22

yaṁ labdhvā cā 'paraṁ lābhaṁ
manyate nā 'dhikaṁ tataḥ
yasmin sthito na duḥkhena
guruṇā 'pi vicālyate

23

taṁ vidyād duḥkhasaṁyoga-
viyogaṁ yogasamjñitam
sa niścayena yoktavyo
yogo 'nirviṇṇacetasā

24

saṁkalpaprabhavān kāmāṁs
tyaktvā sarvān aśeṣataḥ
manasai 've 'ndriyagrāmaṁ
viniyamya samantataḥ

25

śanaiḥ-śanair uparamed
buddhyā dhṛtigṛhītayā
ātmasaṁsthaṁ manaḥ kṛtvā
na kiṁcid api cintayet

21

in which infinite joy, through the intellect experienced, beyond the senses,
he knows; and in which established, he surely does not move from truth;

22

and gaining which, no other gain he considers as greater than that;
wherein founded, no grief, even the heaviest, shakes him:

23

that, know—the disunion from union with pain—to be absorption in yoga;
this, with conviction, practise: yoga, with an undismayed heart.

24

will-spawned desires, all, renouncing entirely;
with the mind, the host of senses surely restraining, on every side;

25

by degrees growing still, through firmly restraining the intellect;
in the soul having established the mind, let him not think of anything.

26

yato-yato niścarati
manaś cañcalam asthiram
tatas-tato niyamyai 'tad
ātmany eva vaśam nayet

27

praśantamanasaṁ hy enaṁ
yoginaṁ sukham uttamam
upaiti śāntarajasaṁ
brahmabhūtam akalmaṣam

28

yuñjann evaṁ sadā 'tmānaṁ
yogī vigatakalmaṣaḥ
sukhena brahmasaṁsparśam
atyantaṁ sukham aśnute

29

sarvabhūtastham ātmānaṁ
sarvabhūtāni cā 'tmani
īkṣate yogayuktātmā
sarvatra samadarśanaḥ

30

yo māṁ paśyati sarvatra
sarvaṁ ca mayi paśyati
tasyā haṁ na pranaśyāmi
sa ca me na praṇaśyati

26

wherever the restless and fickle mind strays, from there it must be restrained,
brought back under the sway of just the atman.

27

who is of serene mind, only to this yogi the highest bliss
comes, his passion stilled, his spirit in brahman, sinless.

28

thus constantly devoting himself, the yogi, delivered from sin,
easily communes with brahman, enjoys infinite bliss.

29

in all beings the atman, and all beings in the soul:
the one absorbed in yoga sees everywhere the same.

30

who sees me everywhere, and everything sees in me,
to him i am never lost, and he is not lost to me.

31

sarvabhūtasthitaṁ yo māṁ
bhajaty ekatvam āsthitaḥ
sarvathā vartamāno 'pi
sa yogī mayi vartate

32

ātmaupamyena sarvatra
samaṁ paśyati yo 'rjuna
sukhaṁ vā yadi vā duḥkhaṁ
sa yogī paramo mataḥ

33

arjuna uvāca
yo 'yaṁ yogas tvayā proktaḥ
sāmyena madhusūdana
etasyā 'haṁ na paśyāmi
cañcalatvāt sthitiṁ sthirām

34

cañcalaṁ hi manaḥ kṛṣṇa
pramāthi balavad dṛḍham
tasyā haṁ nigrahaṁ manye
vāyor iva suduṣkaram

35

śrībhagavān uvāca
asaṁśayaṁ mahābāho
mano durnigrahaṁ calam
abhyāsena tu kaunteya
vairāgyeṇa ca gṛhyate

31

as abiding in all beings, who worships me, founded in oneness,
whatever his life, he is a yogi and lives in me.

32

in the image of himself, who everywhere sees the same,
arjuna, be it in pleasure or in pain, he is deemed the highest yogi.

33

arjuna said:
this yoga you have said to be sameness, madhusudana,
for this i see no enduring stability—out of restlessness.*

34

fickle, surely, is the mind, krishna, turbulent, strong, obstinate;
to control it, i think, is so difficult—like** the wind.

35

the gracious lord said:
doubtless, mahabaho, the mind is difficult to control, unsteady;
but with practice, kaunteya, and dispassion, it is restrained.

---

*of mind.

**controlling.

36

asaṁyatātmanā yogo
duṣprāpa iti me matih
vaśyātmanā tu yatatā
śakyo 'vāptum upāyataḥ

37

arjuna uvāca
ayatiḥ śraddhayo 'peto
yogāc calitamānasaḥ
aprāpya yogasaṁsiddhiṁ
kāṁ gatiṁ kṛṣṇa gacchati

38

kaccin no 'bhayavibhraṣṭas
chinnābhram iva naśyati
apratiṣṭho mahābāho
vimūḍho brahmaṇaḥ pathi

39

etan me saṁśayaṁ kṛṣṇa
chettum arhasy aśeṣataḥ
tvadanyaḥ saṁśayasyā 'sya
chettā na hy upapadyate

40

śrībhagavān uvāca
pārtha nai 've 'ha nā 'mutra
vināśas tasya vidyate
na hi kalyāṇakṛt kaścid
durgatiṁ tāta gacchati

36

for the unrestrained, yoga is difficult to attain, i agree;
but the restrained soul, striving expediently, can attain it.

37

arjuna said:
who cannot control himself, though he has faith, whose mind strays from yoga,
without attaining consummation in yoga, to what end, krishna, does he come?

38

does he not, from both fallen,* and like a rent cloud, surely perish,
unstable, mahabaho, confounded along the path of brahman?

39

this my doubt, krishna, you must dispel entirely;
none but you, for sure, can effect the undoing of this doubt.

40

the gracious lord said:
partha, neither here nor hereafter, does he find harm;
for never does any good man, my friend, come to evil.

---

*devotion and yoga.

41

prāpya puṇyakṛtāṁ lokān
uṣitvā śāśvatīḥ samāḥ
śucīnāṁ śrīmatāṁ gehe
yogabhraṣṭo 'bhijāyate

42

athavā yoginām eva
kule bhavati dhīmatām
etad dhi durlabhataraṁ
loke janma yad īdṛśam

43

tatra taṁ buddhisaṁyogaṁ
labhate paurvadehikam
yatate ca tato bhūyaḥ
saṁsiddhau kurunandana

44

pūrvābhyāsena tenai 'va
hriyate hy avaśo 'pi saḥ
jijñāsur api yogasya
śabdabrahmā 'tivartate

45

prayatnād yatamānas tu
yogī saṁśuddhakilbiṣaḥ
anekajanmasaṁsiddhas
tato yāti parāṁ gatim

41

having attained worlds of the righteous, living there for countless years,
into a home of the pious and the prosperous, the one fallen from yoga is nobly born.

42

else, born even into a family of yogis of wisdom;
though rare indeed in the world is such a birth.

43

thereupon, the evolution of his past life he recovers;
and, with that, strives again for perfection, kurunandana.*

44

also, that same previous practice bears him away, inexorably;
even a seeker after yoga transcends the veda.†

45

but the yogi who strives with zealous mind, purified of all sin,
through many lives perfected, then comes to the supreme.

---

*joy, child of the kurus.

†vedic ritual.

46

tapasvibhyo 'dhiko yogī
jñānibhyo 'pi mato 'dhikaḥ
karmibhyaś cā 'dhiko yogī
tasmād yogī bhavā 'rjuna

47

yoginām api sarveṣāṁ
madgatenā 'ntarātmanā
śraddhāvān bhajate yo māṁ
sa me yuktatamo mataḥ

46

than the tapasvin* greater the yogi; also greater than the gyani,† regarded;
than the karmi‡ greater the yogi—so a yogi become, arjuna.

47

of all yogis, even, who abides in me in his inmost soul, who devotedly worships me, him i consider the foremost yukta.

this is the sixth canto of the srimad bhagavad gita named dhyana yoga

---

*ascetic.
†man of knowledge, wisdom.
‡man of deeds, work.

canto 7

the way of knowledge and realisation

1

śrībhagavān uvāca
mayy āsaktamanāḥ pārtha
yogaṁ yuñjan madāśrayaḥ
asaṁśayaṁ samagraṁ māṁ
yathā jñāsyasi tac chṛṇu

2

jñānaṁ te 'haṁ savijñānam
idaṁ vakṣyāmy aśeṣataḥ
yaj jñātvā ne 'ha bhūyo 'nyaj
jñātavyam avaśiṣyate

3

manuṣyāṇāṁ sahasreṣu
kaścid yatati siddhaye
yatatām api siddhānāṁ
kaścin māṁ vetti tattvataḥ

4

bhūmir āpo 'nalo vāyuh
khaṁ mano buddhir eva ca
ahaṁkāra itī 'yaṁ me
bhinnā prakṛtir aṣṭadhā

5

apare 'yam itas tv anyāṁ
prakṛtiṁ viddhi me parām
jīvabhūtāṁ mahābāho
yahye 'daṁ dhāryate jagat

1

the gracious lord said:
to me the mind cleaving, partha, devoted in yoga, taking refuge in me,
without doubt, you will know me in full—listen how.

2

this knowledge to you, i, together with wisdom, will tell in full,
which knowing, nothing else here will remain to be known.

3

among thousands of men scarcely one strives for perfection;
among these seekers, even among sages,* hardly one knows me in truth.

4

earth, water, fire, air, ether, mind, intellect and also ego—this my differentiated nature, eightfold.

5

this is my lower nature; know my other transcendent nature—the *living spirit*, mahabaho, which supports this world.

---

*siddhas: the perfect. a siddha is also a semi-divine being of great purity, characterised by eight supernatural faculties, or siddhis.

6

etadyonīni būtāni
sarvāṇī 'ty upadhāraya
ahaṁ kṛtsnasya jagataḥ
prabhavaḥ pralayas tathā

7

mattaḥ parataraṁ nā 'nyat
kiṁcid asti dhanaṁjaya
mayi sarvam idaṁ protaṁ
sūtre maṇigaṇā iva

8

raso 'ham apsu kaunteya
prabhā 'smi śaśisūryayoḥ
praṇavaḥ sarvavedeṣu
śabdaḥ khe pauruṣaṁ nṛṣu

9

puṇyo gandhaḥ pṛithivyāṁ ca
tejaś cā 'smi vibhāvasau
jīvanaṁ sarvabhūteṣu
tapaś cā 'smi tapasviṣu

10

bījaṁ māṁ sarvabhūtānāṁ
viddhi pārtha sanātanam
buddhir buddhimatām asmi
tejas tejasvinām aham

6

these two are the womb of all beings, know;
i am all the world's source and its dissolution, as well.

7

than me higher nothing else at all exists, dhananjaya;
in* me all this is strung like so many jewels on a thread.

8

taste am i in water, kaunteya; light i am in moon and sun;
aum in all the vedas, sound in ether, manliness in men.

9

the pure fragrance in the earth i am, and brilliance in fire;
life in all beings am i, and austerity in ascetics.

10

the seed am i of all creatures, know, partha—eternal;
the intelligence of the intelligent i am; the splendour of the splendid, i.

---

*on me.

11

balaṁ balavatāṁ cā 'haṁ
kāmarāgavivarjitam
dharmāviruddho bhūteṣu
kāmo 'smi bharatarṣabha

12

ye cai 'va sāttvikā bhāvā
rājasās tāmasāś ca ye
matta eve 'ti tān viddhi
na tv ahaṁ teṣu te mayi

13

tribhir guṇamayair bhāvair
ebhiḥ sarvam idaṁ jagat
mohitaṁ 'nā bhijānāli
maṁ ebhyaḥ param avyayam

14

daivī hy eṣā guṇamayī
mama māyā duratyayā
mām eva ye prapadyante
māyām etāṁ taranti te

15

na māṁ duṣkṛtino mūḍhāḥ
prapadyante narādhamāḥ
māyayā 'pahṛtajñānā
āsuraṁ bhāvam āśritāḥ

11

and i am the strength of the strong; of lust, passion devoid;
in beings, legitimate desire am i, bharatarishabha.

12

and whatever sattvik existences, of rajas and tamas there are:
from me alone they are, know—i am not in them; they are in me.

13

by all these, the three gunas' manifestations, this whole world,
deluded, does not know me, transcendent, supreme, immutable.

14

for, this divine, guna-comprised maya of mine is impenetrable;
only who in me refuge, they cross over this maya.

15

not in me evil-doers, fools, refuge, lowest of men;
robbed by maya of wisdom, they yield to demonic ways.

16

calurvidhā bhajante māṁ
janāḥ sukṛtino 'rjuna
ārto jijñāsur arthārthī
jñānī ca bharatarṣabha

17

teṣāṁ jñānī nityayukta
ekabhaktir viśiṣyate
priyo hi jñānino 'tyartham
ahaṁ sa ca mama priyaḥ

18

udārāḥ sarva evai 'te
jñānī tv ātmai 'va me matam
āsthitaḥ sa hi yuktātmā
mām evā 'nuttamāṁ gatim

19

bahūnāṁ janmanām ante
jñānavān māṁ prapadyate
vāsudevaḥ sarvam iti
sa mahātmā sudurlabhaḥ

20

kāmais tais-tair hṛtajñānāḥ
prapadyante 'nyadevatāḥ
taṁ-taṁ niyamam āsthāya
prakṛtyā niyatāḥ svayā

16

four kinds of men worship me, virtuous ones, arjuna:
the distressed, the aspirant,* the material seeker,† and the wise man, bharatarishabha.

17

of these the wise man, always in communion, of singular devotion, is the best;
for, most dear to the wise man i am, and he is dear to me.

18

noble are all these, surely, but the gyani i regard as my own self;
because he, the yoked soul, is absorbed just in me, as his highest refuge.

19

at the end of many lives, the wise man resorts to me:
'*because vasudeva is all*'—such a great soul is exceedingly rare.

20

through desire they whose wisdom is swayed, worship other gods,
a myriad of rites observing, by their own natures compelled.

---

*after knowledge; the spiritual seeker.
†of wealth, gain.

21

yo-yo yāṁ-yāṁ tanuṁ bhaktaḥ
śraddhayā 'rcitum icchati
tasya-tasyā calāṁ śraddhāṁ
tām eva vidadhāmy aham

22

sa tayā śraddhayā yuktas
tasyā rādhanam īhate
labhate ca tataḥ kāmān
mayai 'va vihitān hi tān

23

antavat tu phalaṁ teṣāṁ
tad bhavaty alpamedhasām
devān devayajo yānti
madbhaktā yānti mām api

24

avyaktaṁ vyaktim āpannaṁ
manyante mām abuddhayaḥ
paraṁ bhāvam ajānanto
mamā 'vyayam anuttamam

25

nā 'haṁ prakāśaḥ sarvasya
yogamāyāsamāvṛtaḥ
mūḍho 'yaṁ nā 'bhijānāti
loko mām ajam avyayam

21

whatever form, however, any devotee wishes to worship with faith,
in just that his faith i make firm.

22

he, to this faith yoked, that* to propitiate seeks;
and through that, obtains his wishes, which in truth by me alone are granted.

23

but they have an end, the fruits of these small-minded ones;
to the devas, the worshippers of devas go; and my devotees come to me.

24

the unmanifest as reduced into manifestation, the ignorant regard me;
my supreme nature not knowing—imperishable, unsurpassed.

25

i am not plain to all, being cloaked by my yogamaya;
this foolish world does not know me: un-born, immortal.

---

*form, deity.

26

vedā 'haṁ samatītāni
vartamānān cā 'rjuna
bhaviṣyāṇi ca bhūtāni
māṁ tu veda na kaścana

27

icchādveṣasamutthena
dvandvamohena bhārata
sarvabhūtāni saṁmohaṁ
sarge yānti paraṁtapa

28

yeṣāṁ tv antagataṁ pāpaṁ
janānāṁ puṇyakarmaṇām
te dvaṁdvamohanirmuktā
bhajante māṁ dṛḍhavratāḥ

29

jarāmaraṇamokṣāya
mām āśritya yatanti ye
te brahma tad viduḥ kṛtsnam
adhyātmaṁ karma cā 'khilam

30

sādhibhūtādhidaivaṁ māṁ
sādhiyajñaṁ ca ye viduḥ
pravāṇakāle 'pi ca māṁ
te vidur yuktacetasah

26

i know equally, arjuna, past and present
and future beings; but me no one knows.

27

by desire- and aversion-arisen duality seduced, bhaarata,
all creatures are born to ignorance, parantapa.

28

but whose sins have come to an end, men of virtuous deeds:
they, from duality's delusion freed, worship me with unswerving devotion.

29

for liberation from decay, death, who strive, sheltering in me,
they the brahman truly know, the atman entirely, and all about karma.

30

as the lord of creatures,* master of gods, the support of sacrifice, me who know,
with absorbed minds they also know me even at the hour of death.

this is the seventh canto of the srimad bhagavad gita named gyana vigyana yoga

---

*the elements, the material world.

canto 8

the way of immortal brahman

1

arjuna uvāca
kiṁ tad brahma kim adhyātmaṁ
kiṁ karma puruṣottama
adhibhūtaṁ ca kiṁ proktam
adhidaivaṁ kim ucyate

2

adhiyajñaḥ kathaṁ ko 'tra
dehe 'smin madhusūdana
prayāṇakāle ca kathaṁ
jñeyo 'si niyatātmabhiḥ

3

śrībhagavān uvāca
akṣaraṁ brahma paramaṁ
svabhāvo dhyātmam ucyate
bhūtabhāvodbhavakaro
visargaḥ karmasaṁjñitaḥ

4

adhibhūtaṁ kṣaro bhāvaḥ
puruṣaś cā 'dhidaivatam
adhiyajño 'ham evā 'tra
dehe dehabhṛtāṁ vara

5

antakāle ca mām eva
smaran muktvā kalevaram
yaḥ prayāti sa madbhāvaṁ
yāti nā 'sty atra saṁśayaḥ

1

arjuna said:

what is that brahman, what adhyatma,* what karma, purushottama?

and what is called adhibhootam, what said to be adhidaivam?

2

who is the adhiyagna, and how: here in this body, madhusudana?

and at the hour of death how are you known by the restrained soul?

3

the gracious lord said:

deathless brahman is supreme; nature is called adhyatmam;

beings, souls, that which creates, sends forth, is named karma.

4

adhibhootam is mortal forms, and purusha,** adhidaivatam;

adhiyagna even i am, in this body, o most excellent of the living.

5

and at the time of the end, only me remembering,

while leaving the body, who departs, he comes to my being: of this there is no doubt.

---

*the supreme soul.

**the cosmic person.

6

yaṁ-yaṁ vā 'pi smaran bhāvaṁ
tyajaty ante kalevaram
taṁ-tam evai 'ti kaunteya
sadā tadbhāvabhāvitaḥ

7

tasmāt sarveṣu kālesu
mām anusmara yudhya ca
mayy arpitamanobuddhir
mām evai 'syasy asaṁśayaḥ

8

abhyāsayogayuktena
cetasā nā 'nyagāminā
paramaṁ puruṣaṁ divyaṁ
yāti pārthā 'nucintayan

9

kaviṁ purāṇam anuśāsitāram
aṇor aṇīyāṁsam anusmared yaḥ
sarvasya dhātāram acintyarūpam
ādityavarṇaṁ tamasaḥ parastāt

10

prayāṇakāle manasā 'calena
bhaktyā yukto yogabalena cai 'va
bhruvor madhye prāṇam āveśya samyak
sa taṁ paraṁ puruṣam upaiti divyam

6
or else, of whatever thinking he gives up the body,
even to that he surely attains, kaunteya, being ever
absorbed in that thought.

7
so, at all times, think of me, and fight;
to me your heart and mind offered, to me you will
surely come, without doubt.

8
mind engaged in absorption in yoga, not straying,
who meditates, partha, the supreme purusha, divine,
attains.

9
who meditates on the seer, the ancient, the ruler,
smaller than the smallest,
the support of everything, of inconceivable form, sun-
coloured, beyond darkness,

10
at the hour of death, mind stilled, with devotion, yoked,
and also, with the power of yoga,
prana fixed firmly between the brows—he, that supreme
purusha attains, divine.

11

yad akṣaraṁ vedavido vadanti
viśanti yad yatayo vītarāgāḥ
yad icchanto brahmacaryaṁ caranti
tat te padaṁ saṁgraheṇa pravakṣye

12

sarvadvārāṇi saṁyamya
mano kṛdi nirudhya ca
mūrdhny ādhāyā 'tmanah prāṇam
āsthito yogadhāraṇām

13

aum ity ekākṣaraṁ brahma
vyāharan mām anusmaran
yaḥ prayāti tyajan dehaṁ
sa yāti paramāṁ gatim

14

ananyacetāḥ satataṁ
yo māṁ smarati nityaśaḥ
tasyā 'haṁ sulabhaḥ pārtha
nityayuktasya yoginaḥ

15

mām upetya punarjanma
duhkhālayam aśāśvatam
nā pnuvanti mahātmānaḥ
saṁsiddhiṁ paramāṁ gatāḥ

11

that *immortal* of which veda knowers speak, which passionless sages enter;
wanting which, they practice brahmacharya—that condition to you briefly i will tell.

12

all inlets* restrained, and the mind confined in the heart;
in the head fixing the soul's life-breath, founded firm in yoga,

13

aum, the one-syllabled brahman, uttering, remembering me,
who departs, leaving the body, he goes to the highest destination.

14

of nothing else aware, who ever remembers me, with constancy,
to him i am attainable, partha, to the always yoked yogi.

15

attaining me, to rebirth, house of sorrow, impermanent,
great souls do not return—the highest perfection they have reached.

---

*of the body, the senses.

16

ā brahmabhuvanāl lokāḥ
punarāvartino 'rjuna
mām upetya tu kaunteya
punarjanma na vidyate

17

sahasrayugaparyantam
ahar yad brahmaṇo viduḥ
rātriṁ yugasahasrāntām
te 'horātravido janāḥ

18

avyaktād vyaktayaḥ sarvāḥ
prabhavanty aharāgame
rātryāgame pralīyante
tatrai vā 'vyaktasamjñake

19

bhūtagrāmaḥ sa evā 'yaṁ
bhūtvā-bhūtvā pralīyate
rātryāgame 'vaśaḥ pārtha
prabhavaty aharāgame

20

paras tasmāt tu bhāvo 'nyo
'vyakto 'vyaktāt sanātanaḥ
yaḥ sa sarveṣu bhūteṣu
naśyatsu na vinaśyati

16

up to brahma's realm, all worlds are subject to rebirth, arjuna;
but upon me attaining, kaunteya, there is no experiencing birth again.

17

a thousand yugas lasts brahma's day, who know,
that his night lasts a thousand yugas, they are knowers of day and night.

18

from the unmanifest all the manifest come forth at the advent of day;*
at the coming of night, they then dissolve into that same, called the unmanifest.

19

the host of beings, they the same which recur, dissolves, when night comes, helplessly, partha, comes forth, when day arrives.

20

but beyond this existence is another unmanifest unmanifestation eternal:
he who, when all beings perish, is not destroyed.

*brahma's day.

21

avyakto 'kṣara ity uktas
tam āhuḥ paramāṁ gatim
yaṁ prāpya na nivartante
tad dhāma paramaṁ mama

22

puruṣaḥ sa paraḥ pārtha
bhaktyā labhyas tv ananyayā
yasyā 'ntaḥsthāni bhūtāni
yena sarvam idaṁ tatam

23

yatra kāle tv anāvṛttim
āvṛttiṁ cai 'va yoginaḥ
prayātā yānti taṁ kālaṁ
vakṣyāmi bharatarṣabha

24

agnir jyotir ahaḥ śuklah
ṣaṇmāsā uttarāyaṇam
tatra prayātā gacchanti
brahma brahmavido janāḥ

25

dhūmo rātris tathā kṛṣṇaḥ
ṣaṇmāsā dakṣiṇāyanam
tatra cāndramasaṁ jyotir
yogī prāpya nivartate

21

this unmanifest is said to be imperishable: *this*, which is called the supreme condition,
whom attaining, they do not return—that is my supreme abode.

22

he is the supreme purusha, partha, but through singular devotion can be attained—
in whom all beings dwell, by whom all this is pervaded.

23

now the times of yogis not returning, and also returning,
when departing hence—those times i will tell you, bharatarishabha.

24

fire, light, day, the bright fortnight,* the northern course:†
by these departing, those who know brahman to brahman go.

25

smoke, night, also the dark fortnight, the six months of the southern course:
there, the lunar light, the yogi, obtaining, returns.

---

*when the moon waxes.

†the six months of the sun's northern course.

26

śuklakṛṣṇe gatī hy ete
jagataḥ śāśvate mate
ekayā yāty anāvṛittim
anyayā 'vartate punaḥ

27

nai 'te sṛtī pārtha jānan
yogī muhyati kaścana
tasmāt sarveśu kāleṣu
yogayukto bhavā 'rjuna

28

vedeṣu yajñeṣu tapaḥsu cai 'va
dāneṣu yat puṇyaphalaṁ pradiṣṭam
atyeti tat sarvaṁ idaṁ viditvā
yogī paraṁ sthānam upaiti cā 'dyam

26

the bright, the dark: surely these paths of the world are considered eternal;
going by one, he does not return; by the other he comes back again.

27

not, these paths, partha, knowing, is the yogi deluded, ever;
so, at all times, yoked in yoga be, arjuna.

28

by the veda, by sacrifice, through penance, and also from charity what good fruits accrue—
the yogi transcends all that, and, this knowing, the supreme place attains, the primeval.

this is the eighth canto of the srimad bhagavad gita named aksharabrahma yoga.

canto 9

the way of royal knowledge, the royal secret

1

śrībhagavān uvāca
idaṁ tu te guhyatamaṁ
pravakṣyāmy anasūyave
jñānaṁ vijñānasahitaṁ
yaj jñātvā mokṣyase 'śubhāt

2

rājavidyā rājaguhyaṁ
pavitram idam uttamam
pratyakṣāvagamaṁ dharmyaṁ
susukhaṁ kartum avyayam

3

aśraddahānāḥ puruṣā
dharmasyā 'sya paraṁtapa
aprāpya māṁ nivartante
mṛtyusaṁsāravartmani

4

mayā tatam idaṁ sarvaṁ
jagad avyaktamūrtinā
matsthāni sarvabhūtāni
na cā 'haṁ teṣv avasthitaḥ

5

na ca matsthāni bhūtāni
paśya me yogam aiśvaram
bhūtabhṛn na ca bhūtastho
mamā 'tmā bhūtabhāvanaḥ

1

the gracious lord said:
now to you, this deep secret i will reveal, o unenvious,
along with knowledge, wisdom—knowing which, you will be delivered from evil.

2

the sovereign knowledge, sovereign secret, sacred, this, supreme,
directly perceived, righteous, most easily practised, immortal.

3

men who are faithless in this teaching, parantapa,
not attaining me, return to the path of this world of death.*

4

by me is pervaded all this world: in unmanifest form;
in me are all creatures, and not i in them situated.

5

and not in me are the creatures founded—behold my divine yoga!
the support of beings and not founded in the beings,
my soul the beings' source.

---

*samsara is also the world of illusions.

6

ya hā 'kāśasthito ni yaṁ
vāyuḥ sarvatrago mahān
athā sarvāṇi bhūtāni
matsthānī 'ty upadhāraya

7

sarvabhūtāni kaun ya
prakṛtiṁ yānti māmikām
kalpakṣaye punas tāni
kalpādau visṛjāmy aham

8

prakṛtiṁ svām avaṣṭabhya
visṛjāmi punaḥ-punaḥ
bhūtagrāmam imaṁ kṛtsnam
avaśam prakṛter vaśāt

9

na ca māṁ tām karmāṇi
nibadhnanti dhanaṁjaya
ndāsīnavad āsīnam
asaktaṁ teṣu karmasu

10

mayā 'dhyakṣeṇa prakṛtiḥ
sūyate sacarācaram
hetunā 'nena kaunteya
jagad viparivartate

6

as in akasa* is founded, ever, the great wind going everywhere,
even so do all beings in me abide, reflect.

7

all beings, kaunteya, into prakriti pass, mine, at kalpa's** end;
again, these, at kalpa's beginning, i send forth.

8

in my own nature resting, i emit, again and again,
this entire host of beings, helpless, in prakriti's sway.

9

and not me do these acts bind, dhananjaya;
as one indifferent i remain, unattached amidst these works.

10

under my rule, nature gives birth to all the moving and the immobile;
because of this, kaunteya, the world revolves.

---

*space, sky, cosmic ether. the fifth element.

**see appendix: note on time.

11

avajānanti māṁ mūḍhā
mānuṣiṁ tanum āśritam
paraṁ bhāvam ajānanto
mama bhūtamaheśvaram

12

moghāśā moghakarmāṇo
moghajñānā vicetasaḥ
rākṣasīm āsurīm cai 'va
prakṛtiṁ mohinīṁ śritāḥ

13

mahātmānas tu māṁ pārtha
daivīṃ prakṛtim āśritāh
bhajanty ananyamanaso
jñātvā bhūtādim avyayam

14

satataṁ kīrtayanto māṁ
yatantaś ca drdhavartāḥ
namasyantaś ca māṁ bhaktyā
nityayuktā upāsate

15

jñanayajñena cā 'py anye
yajanto mām upāsate
ekatvena pṛthaktvena
bahudhā viśvatomukham

11

fools mock me, who have assumed a human body:
my supreme nature not knowing—the great lord of beings.

12

of vain hopes, of vain deeds, of vain knowledge, witless;
and also of rakshasas' and asuras' deluded nature partaking.*

13

but great souls, partha, abiding in divine nature, me worship, single-mindedly,
knowing** the source of beings, imperishable.

14

always hymning me, and striving, with stern vows;
venerating me with devotion, ever yoked, they worship.

15

and through the ritual of wisdom yet others sacrifice, worship me:
as one, as apart, as many, universe-faced.

*those that mock me.

**i am.

16

ahaṁ kratur ahaṁ yajñaḥ
svadhā 'ham aham auṣadham
mantro 'ham aham evā 'jyam
aham agnir ahaṁ hutam

17

pitā 'ham asya jagato
mātā dhātā pitāmahaḥ
vedyaṁ pavitram auṁkāra
ṛk sāma yajur eva ca

18

gatir bhartā prabhuḥ sākṣī
nivāsaḥ śaranaṁ suhṛt
prabhavaḥ pralayaḥ sthānaṁ
nidhānaṁ bījam avyayam

19

tapāmy aham ahaṁ varṣaṁ
nigṛhṇāmy utsṛjāmi ca
amṛtaṁ cai 'va mṛtyuś ca
sad asac cā 'ham arjuna

20

traividyā māṁ somapāḥ pūtapāpā
yajñair iṣṭvā svargatiṁ prārthayante
te puṇyam āsādya surendralokam
aśnanti divyān divi devabhogān

16

i am the ritual; i am sacrifice; the ancestral oblation, i; i, the herb;
the mantra, i; i alone the clarified butter; i, the fire; i, the offering.

17

the father, i, of this world, the mother, supporter, grandsire;
that which is to be known, the purifier, *aum*, rik, sama and yajus, also.

18

the goal, sustainer, lord, witness, abode, refuge, friend;
the origin, dissolution, the ground, the receptacle, the seed eternal.

19

i give heat; i withhold and send forth rain; immortality and death, also, and reality and unreality—i, arjuna.

20

veda-knowers* who drink soma and are cleansed of sin, worshipping me with sacrifices, pray for the passage to heaven;†
they attain the holy world of indra, enjoy in heaven divine pleasures of the gods.

---

*knowers of the three vedas. the atharva is often not included in vaishnava texts.
†svarga.

21

te taṁ bhuktvā svargalokaṁ viśālaṁ
kṣīṇe puṇye martyalokaṁ viśanti
evaṁ trayīdharmam anuprapannā
gatāgat ṁ kāma āmā labhante

22

ananyāś cintayanto māṁ
ye janāḥ paryupāsate
ieṣāṁ nityābhiyuktānāṁ
yogakṣemaṁ vahāmy aham

23

ye 'py anyadevatābhaktā
yajante śraddhayā 'nvitāḥ
le 'pi mām eva kaunteya
yajanty avidhipūrvakam

24

ahaṁ hi sarvayajñānāṁ
bhoktā ca prabhur eva ca
na tu mām abhijānanti
tattvenā 'taś cyavanti te

25

yānti devavratā devān
pitṝn yānti pitṛvratāḥ
bhūtāni yānti bhūtejyā
yānti madyājino 'pi mām

21

they that enjoy the vast world of heaven, when their
merit is exhausted enter the mortal world;
thus, followers of the triune faith, seekers after pleasure,
come and go.

22

with no other thought, they who worship me:
constantly, assiduously, their welfare i support.

23

those, too, other gods' devotees, who sacrifice with faith,
they, also, only to me, kaunteya, sacrifice; not by ancient
law.*

24

for, i of all sacrifices am the enjoyer, and the lord, as
well;
but they do not know me truly; so, they fall.

25

deva worshippers go to the devas;
to the manes go adorers of the pitris;
to spirits go spirit worshippers;
and my worshippers come to me.

*though.

26

pattraṁ puṣpaṁ phalaṁ toyaṁ
yo me bhaktyā prayacchati
tad ahaṁ bhaktyupahṛtam
aśnāmi prayatātmanaḥ

27

yat karosi yad aśnāsi
yaj juhoṣi dadāsi yat
yat tapasyasi kaunteya
tat kuruṣva madarpaṇam

28

śubhāśubhaphalaïr evaṁ
mokṣyase karmabandhanaiḥ
saṁnyāsayogayuktātmā
vimukto mām upaiṣyasi

29

samo 'haṁ sarvabhūteṣu
na me dveṣyo 'sti na priyaḥ
ye bhajanti tu māṁ bhaktyā
mayi te teṣu cā 'py aham

30

api cet sudurācāro
bhajate mām ananyabhāk
sādhur eva sa mantavyaḥ
samyag vyavasito hi saḥ

26

a leaf, flower, fruit, water,
who, to me, with devotion offers:
that devout offering,
of a pious soul, i accept.

27

whatever you do, what you eat, that which you sacrifice;
whatever penance you perform, kaunteya—that make an offering to me.

28

thus from good and bad consequences you will be free,
the bondage of karma;
to renunciation and yoga mind yoked, liberated,
me you will attain.

29

the same, i, to all beings: none to me is hateful, none dear;
but those who worship me with devotion,
they are in me and i, too, in them.

30

if even a most sinful one worships me, single-mindedly,
a saint he must be considered, for he has rightly resolved.

31

kṣipraṁ bhavati dharmātmā
śaśvacchāntiṁ nigacchati
kaunteya pratijānīhi
na me bhaktaḥ praṇaśyati

32

māṁ hi partha vyapāśritya
ye 'pi syuḥ pāpayonayaḥ
striyo vaiśyās tathā śūdrās
te 'pi yānti parām gatim

33

kiṁ punar brāhmaṇāḥ puṇyā
bhaktā rājarṣayas tathā
antiyam asukhaṁ lokam
imaṁ prāpya bhajasva mām

34

manmanā bhava madbhakto
madyājī māṁ namaskuru
mām evai 'ṣyasi yuktvai 'vam
ātmānaṁ matparāyaṇaḥ

31
quickly he becomes a righteous soul, eternal peace attains;
kaunteya, know for certain, never does my bhakta perish.

32
for, in me, partha, those who refuge, even they of sinful birth,
women, vaishyas and sudras, they also attain the supreme goal.

33
how much more then, pure brahmanas and devout royal sages;
this impermanent, unhappy world having found—worship me.

34
your mind on me; be my devotee;
to me sacrifice; to me bow;
to me you will surely come, thus devoted,
your soul on me intent.

this is the ninth canto of the srimad bhagavad gita named rajavidyarajaguhya yoga

canto 10

the way of brahman

1

śrībhagavān uvāca
bhūya eva mahābāho
śṛṇu me paramaṁ vacaḥ
yat te 'haṁ prīyamāṇāya
vakṣyāmi hitakāmyayā

2

na me viduḥ suragaṇaḥ
prabhavaṁ na maharṣayaḥ
aham ādir hi devānāṁ
maharṣīṇāṁ ca sarvaśāḥ

3

yo mām ajam anādiṁ ca
vetti lokamaheśvaram
asaṁmūḍhaḥ sa martyeṣu
sarvapapāiḥ pramucyate

4

buddhir jñānam asaṁmohaḥ
kṣamā satyaṁ damaḥ śamaḥ
sukhaṁ duhkhaṁ bhavo 'bhāvo
bhayaṁ cā 'bhayam eva ca

5

ahiṁsā samata tūstis
tapo dānaṁ yaśo 'yaśaḥ
bhavanti bhāva bhūtānāṁ
matta eva pṛthagvidhāḥ

1

the gracious lord said:
yet again, mighty-armed, hear my supreme word,
which to you, i, holding you dear, will tell, wishing your weal.

2

neither the hosts of devas my origin know, nor the maharishis;
for, i am the source of the devas and the maharishis, in every way.

3

who me, un-born and beginningless, great god of the world, knows—
undeluded, he, among mortals, from all sin liberated.

4

intelligence, knowledge, clarity,
patience, truth, self-control, calm;
joy, sorrow; being, non-being;
and fear and also fearlessness;

5

non-violence, equanimity, contentment, austerity, charity, fame, infamy—
born, these dispositions of beings, from me alone, of different kinds.

6

maharṣayaḥ sapta pūrve
catvāro manavas lathā
madbhāvā mānasā jātā
yeṣāṁ loka imāḥ prajāḥ

7

etāṁ vibhūtiṁ yogaṁ ca
mama yo vetti tattvataḥ
so 'vikampena yogena
yujyate nā 'tra saṁśayaḥ

8

ahaṁ sarvasya prabhavo
mattaḥ sarvaṁ pravartate
iti matvā bhajante māṁ
budhā bhāvasamanvitāḥ

9

maccittā madgataprāṇā
bodhayantaḥ parasparam
kathayantaś ca māṁ nityaṁ
tuṣyanti ca ramanti ca

10

teṣāṁ satatayuktānāṁ
bhajatāṁ prītipūrvakam
dadāmi buddhiyogaṁ taṁ
yena mām upayānti te

6

the great sages, the seven,* and the earlier four;†
the manus, also:
of my being, mind, born—from these,
this world's progeny.

7

this power and work of mine who knows in truth,
he to unfaltering communion is joined—of this, no doubt.

8

i, of all the source; from me everything begins;
this knowing, me the wise worship, with devotion.

9

in me their thought, to me given their life, awakening one another;
and speaking of me always; and contented and joyful.

10

to them, always devoted, worshipping with love,
i give buddhi yoga, by which to me they come.

---

*marichi, atri, angiras, pulastya, pulaha, kratu and vasishta.
†sanatkumara, sanatana, sananda and sanaka.

11

teṣāṁ evā 'nukampārthaṁ
aham ajñānajaṁ tamaḥ
nāśayāmy ātmabhāvastho
jñānadīpena bhāsvatā

12

arjuna uvāca
paraṁ brahma paraṁ dhāma
pavitraṁ paranaṁ bhavān
puruṣaṁ śāśvataṁ divyam
ādidevam ajaṁ vibhum

13

āhus tvām ṛṣayaḥ sarve
devarṣir nāradas tathā
asito devalo vyāsaḥ
svayaṁ cai 'va bravīṣi me

14

sarvam etad ṛtaṁ manye
yan māṁ vadāsi keśava
na hi te bhagavan vyaktiṁ
vidur devā na dānavāḥ

15

svayam evā 'tmanā 'tmānaṁ
vettha tvaṁ puruṣottama
bhūtabhāvana bhūteśa
devadeva jagatpate

11

for these, out of tenderness alone, i their darkness of ignorance,
dwelling in my self dispel, with the lamp of wisdom, resplendent.

12

arjuna said:
the supreme brahman, the highest abode, absolutely pure,
you are, the purusha eternal, divine, the primeval god, un-born, immanent,

13

say all the sages, devarishi narada, too,
asita, devala, vyasa; and you yourself tell me so.

14

all this i hold true, which to me you say, kesava;
not, surely, lord, your origin the devas know, nor the danavas.*

15

only you yourself your soul, with your soul, know, purushottama,
source of beings, lord of beings, god of gods, lord of the world.

---

*asuras, sons of danu.

16

vaktum arhasy aśeṣeṇa
divyā hy ātmavibhūtayaḥ
yābhir vibhūtibhir lokān
imāṁs tvaṁ vyāpya tiṣṭhasi

17

kathaṁ vidyām ahaṁ yogiṁs
tvāṁ sadā paricintayan
keṣu-keṣu ca bhāveṣu
cintyo 'si bhagavan mayā

18

vistareṇā 'tmano yogaṁ
vibhūtiṁ ca janārdana
bhūyaḥ kathaya tṛptir hi
śṛṇvato nā 'sti me 'mṛtam

19

śrībhagavān uvāca
hanta te kathayiṣyāmi
divyā hy ātmavibhūtayaḥ
prādhānyataḥ kuruśreṣṭha
nā 'sty anto vistarasya me

20

aham ātmā guḍākeśa
sarvabhūtāśayasthitaḥ
aham ādiś ca madhyaṁ ca
bhūtānām anta eva ca

16

surely, you alone can tell fully of the divine powers,
with which glories these worlds, you, pervading, abide.

17

how can i know, o yogin, you, with constant contemplation?
and in which various forms are you, lord, to be thought of by me?

18

expatiate again on your power and might, janardana;
for, i am not sated hearing your words, like nectar.

19

the gracious lord said:
yes, i will tell you my divine manifestations,
only those which are main, best of the kurus—there is no end to my extent.

20

i, the soul, gudakesa, in all beings' hearts dwelling,
and i the beginning and middle, and, also, the end of beings.

21

ādityānām ahaṁ viṣṇur
jyotiṣāṁ ravir aṁśumān
marīcir marutām asmi
nakṣatrāṇām ahaṁ śaśī

22

vedānāṁ sāmavedo 'smi
devānām asmi vāsavaḥ
indriyāṇāṁ manaś cā 'smi
bhūtānām asmi cetanā

23

rudrānam śaṁkaraś cā 'smi
vitteśo yakśarakṣasām
vasūnām pāvakaś cā 'smi
meruḥ śikhariṇām aham

24

purodhasāṁ ca mukhyaṁ māṁ
viddhi pārtha bṛhaspatim
senānīnām ahaṁ skandaḥ
sarasām asmi sāgaraḥ

25

maharṣīṇāṁ bhṛgur ahaṁ
girām asmy ekam akṣaram
yajñānāṁ japayajño 'smi
sthāvarānāṁ himālayaḥ

21

of the adityas i am vishnu; of luminaries, the sun, radiant;
marichi of the maruts i am; of stars i am the moon.

22

of vedas, the sama veda am i; of devas, i am vasavah;*
and of senses the mind, i; in beings i am consciousness.

23

of rudras, shankara i am; vittesha† among yakshas and rakshasas;
and of vasus i am fire; meru among mountains, i.

24

and of priests, the chief, i, know, partha: brihaspati;
of generals, i am skanda; of lakes, i am the ocean.

25

of maharishis, bhrigu, i; of speech, the single syllable;**
of sacrifices the japa yagna†† i am; of mountains, himalaya.

---

*indra.
†kubera.
**aum.
††chanting god's names.

26

aśvatthaḥ sarvavṛkṣāṇāṁ
devarṣīnāṁ ca nāradaḥ
gandharvāṇāṁ citrarathaḥ
siddhānāṁ kapilo munih

27

uccaiḥśravasam aśvānāṁ
viddhi mām amṛtodbhavam
airāvataṁ gajendrāṇāṁ
narāṇāṁ ca narādhipam

28

āyudhānām ahaṁ vajraṁ
dhenūnām asmi kāmadhuk
prajanaś cā 'smi kandarpaḥ
sarpāṇāṁ asmi vāsukiḥ

29

anantaś cā 'smi nāgānāṁ
varuṇo yādasām aham
pitṛnām aryamā cā 'smi
yamaḥ saṁyamatām aham

30

prahlādaś cā 'smi daityānāṁ
kālaḥ kalayatām aham
mṛgāṇāṁ ca mṛgendro 'haṁ
vainateyaś ca pakṣiṇāṁ

26

the aswattha among all trees, and of devarishis narada;
of gandharvas chitraratha; among siddhas, kapila muni.

27

ucchaisravas among horses, know me to be, nectar-born;
airavata among elephant lords, and among men, the king.

28

of weapons, i, the vajra; of cows am i kamadhenu;
and among progenitors, i am kandarpa;*
of serpents i am vasuki.

29

and ananta i am among nagas; varuna of ocean-dwellers, i;
and of the manes aryaman am i; yama of regulators, i.

30

and prahlada i am of daityas;† time, of reckoners;
and of beasts, the king of beasts, i, and vainata‡ of birds.

---

*kama, god of love.

†demons, sons of diti.

‡vinata's son, garuda.

31

pavanaḥ pavatām asmi
rāmaḥ śastrabhṛtām aham
jhaṣāṇāṁ makaraś cā 'smi
srotasām asmi jāh navī

32

sargāṇāṁ ādir antaś ca
madhyaṁ cai 'vā 'ham arjuna
adhyātmavidyā vidyānāṁ
vādaḥ pravadatām aham

33

aksarānam akāro smi
dvandvah samasikasya ca
aham eva kṣayah kālo
dhātā ham viśvatomukhaḥ

34

mṛtyuḥ sarvaharaś cā 'ham
udbhavaś ca bhaviṣyatām
kīrtih srir vāk ca nārīnām
smṛtir medhā dhṛtiḥ kṣamā

35

brhatsāma tathā sāmnāṁ
gāiyatrī chandasām aham
māsānāṁ mārgaśīrso ham
ṛtūnāṁ kusumākaraḥ

31

the wind among purifiers i am; rama of weapon-bearers, i;
and among fish the crocodile i am; among rivers i am jaahnavi.*

32

of creations, the beginning and end, also the middle, i, arjuna;
metaphysics of sciences, the dialectic of debators, i.

33

of alphabets, the *a* am i and of compounds, the dual;
i alone, eternal time; the creator, i, facing everywhere.

34

and death, taking all, i, and the source of what is to be;
fame, fortune, speech of women, memory, intelligence, fortitude, patience.

35

the brihat saman, also, of hymns, the gayatri among metres, i;
of months, margasirsa, i; of seasons, the flower-mine.**

---

*ganga.
**spring.

36

dyūtaṁ chalayatām asmi
tejas tejasvinam aham
jayo 'smi vyavasāyo 'smi
sattvaṁ sattvavatām aham

37

vrsnīnāṁ vāsudevo 'smi
pāṇḍavānāṁ dhanamjayah
muninam apy aham vyāsaḥ
kavīnām uśanā kaviḥ

38

dando damayatām asmi
nītir asmi jigīṣatam
maunaṁ cai 'vā 'smi guhyānām
jñānaṁ jñānavatam aham

39

yac cā 'pi sarvabhūtānāṁ
bījaṁ tad aham arjuna
na tad asti vinā yat syān
mayā bhūtam carācaram

40

nā 'nto 'sti mama divyānāṁ
vibhūtīnām paraṁtapa
esa tū ddeśatah prokto
vibhūter vistaro mayā

36

of deceivers, gambling i am; the splendour of the splendid, i;
victory i am; effort i am; the goodness of the good, i.

37

of vrisnis, vaasudeva* i am;
of the pandavas, dhananjaya;
of sages vyasa, also, i;
of poets, the poet usana.†

38

the rod,‡ of punishers i am;
the strategy i am of conquest seekers;
and the silence, also, i am, of secrets;
the wisdom of the wise, i.

39

and, further, what is the seed of all beings—that, i, arjuna;
which can exist without me: there can be no being, moving or unmoving.

40

no end is there to my divine manifestations, parantapa;
all this that i have said are illustrative** of my infinite glories.

---

*vasudeva's son, krishna.
†shukra.
‡yama's danda, rod of chastisement.
**merely examples.

41

yad-yad vibhūtimat sattvaṁ
śrīmad ūrjitam eva vā
tat tad evā 'vagaccha tvaṁ
mama tejomśasaṁbhavam

42

athavā bahunai 'tena
kiṁ jñātena tavā 'rjuna
viṣṭabhyā 'ham idam kṛstnam
ekāṁśena sthito jagat

41

whatever existence is glorious, graceful or powerful,
surely,
that, know you, from a portion of my splendour is born.

42

anyway, of what avail all these knowing, to you, arjuna?
i pervade all this with an iota of myself, support the
universe.

this is the tenth canto of the srimad bhagavad gita named vibhutih yoga

canto 11

the yoga of the vision of the cosmic form

1

arjuna uvāca
madanugrahāya paramaṁ
guhyam adhyātmasaṁjñitam
yat tvayo 'ktaṁ vacas tena
moho 'yaṁ vigato mama

2

bhavāpyayau hi bhūtānāṁ
śrutau vistaraśo mayā
tvattaḥ kamalapattrākṣa
māhātmyam api cā 'vyayam

3

evam etad yathā 'ttha tvam
ātmānaṁ parameśvara
draṣṭum icchāmi te rūpam
aiśvaraṁ puruṣottama

4

manyase yadi tac chakyaṁ
mayā draṣṭum iti prabho
yogeśvara tato me tvaṁ
darśayā 'tmānam avyayam

5

śrībhagavān uvāca
paśya me pārtha rūpāṇi
śataśo 'tha sahasraśaḥ
nānāvidhāni divyāni
nānāvarṇākṛtīni ca

1

arjuna said:
to bless me, the supreme, secret, adhyatmam, you revealed;
with these words that you spoke, my bewilderment has gone.

2

indeed, of the appearance and passing of beings, i have heard extensively
from you, lotus-eyed; and also your greatness, imperishable.

3

it is just so: what you have said about yourself, parameswara—
i want to see your *form divine*, purushottama!

4

if you think *that* can be seen by me, lord,
yogeswara, then, to me show your self eternal.

5

the gracious lord said:
behold, partha, my forms, hundreds and thousands,
of many kinds, divine, vari-coloured and -shaped.

6

paśyā 'dityān vasūn rudrān
aśvinau marutas tathā
bahūny adṛṣṭapūrvāṇi
paśyā 'ścaryāṇi bhārata

7

ihai 'kasthaṁ jagat kṛtsnaṁ
paśyā 'dya sacarācaram
mama dehe guḍākeśa
yac cā 'nyad draṣṭum icchasi

8

na tu māṁ śakyase draṣṭum
anenai 'va svacakṣuṣā
divyaṁ dadāmi te cakṣuḥ
paśya me yogam aiśvaram

9

saṁjaya uvāca
evam uktvā tato rājan
mahāyogeśvaro hariḥ
darśayām āsu pārthāya
paramaṁ rūpam aiśvaram

10

anekavaktranayanam
anekādbhutadarśanam
anekadivyābharaṇaṁ
divyānekodyatāyudham

6

behold the adityas, vasus, rudras, the two asvins, also the maruts;
many previously unseen wonders, behold, bhaarata.

7

here, as one, the universe, whole, see now, moving and immobile,
in my body, gudakesa; and whatever else you wish to see.

8

but you cannot see *me* with just these your eyes;
i give you divine sight—behold my sovereign yoga.

9

sanjaya said:
so saying, then, my king, the great lord of yoga, hari,
showed partha his supreme form divine.

10

countless mouths, eyes; countless amazing visions;
countless divine ornaments; countless divine weapons raised;

11

divyamālyāmbaradharaṁ
divyagandhānulepanam
sarvāścaryamayaṁ devam
anantaṁ viśvatomukham

12

divi sūryasahasrasya
bhaved yugapad utthitā
yadi bhāḥ sadṛśī sā syād
bhāsas tasya mahātmanaḥ

13

tatrai 'kasthaṁ jagat kṛtsnaṁ
pravibhaktam anekadhā
apaśyad devadevasya
śarīre pāṇḍavas tadā

14

tataḥ sa vismayāviṣṭo
hṛṣṭaromā dhanaṁjayaḥ
praṇamya śirasā devaṁ
kṛtāñjalir abhāṣata

15

arjuna uvāca
paśyāmi devāṁs tava deva dehe
sarvāṁs thatā bhūtaviśeṣasaṁghān
brahmāṇam īśaṁ kamalāsanastham
ṛṣīṁś ca sarvān uragāṁś ca divyān

11

divine garlands, raiment, wearing;
with divine perfumes anointed;
of all wonders, refulgent;
infinite, faces everywhere.

12

in the sky, if a thousand suns were together risen,
light like that might perhaps compare with the
splendour of that *great being*.

13

there, as one, the universe, whole, of divisions manifold,
saw, in the god of gods' body, then, the pandava.

14

then, he, wonderstruck, horripilating, dhananjaya,
bowing his head before *god*, with hands folded, spoke.

15

arjuna said:
i see the devas, o god, in your body, and also all the
myriad hosts of beings,
brahma, the lord upon lotus-throne seated, and all the
rishis and uragas* divine.

---

*serpents.

16

anekabāhūdaravaktranetraṁ
paśyāmi tvāṁ sarvato 'nantarūpam
nā 'ntaṁ na madhyaṁ na punas tavā 'diṁ
paśyāmi viśveśvara viśvarūpa

17

kirīṭinaṁ gadinaṁ cakriṇaṁ ca
tejorāśiṁ sarvato dīptimantam
paśyāmi tvāṁ durnirīkṣyaṁ samantād
dīptānalārkadyutim aprameyam

18

tvam akṣaraṁ paramaṁ veditavyaṁ
tvam asya viśvasya paraṁ nidhānam
tvam avyayaḥ śāśvatadharmagoptā
sanātanas tvaṁ puruṣo mato me

19

anādimadhyāntam anantavīryam
anantabāhuṁ śaśisūryanetram
paśyāmi tvāṁ dīptahutāśavaktraṁ
svatejasā viśam idaṁ tapantam

20

dyāvāpṛthivyor idam antaraṁ hi
vyāptaṁ tvayai 'kena diśaś ca sarvāḥ
dṛṣṭvā 'dbhutaṁ rūpam ugraṁ tave 'daṁ
lokatrayaṁ pravyathitaṁ mahātman

16

with countless arms, bellies, mouths, eyes: i see your infinite form everywhere;
neither your end nor middle, nor again your beginning, do i see, lord of the universe, o universe-formed.

17

with crowns, maces, and chakras, a mass of light, everywhere shining,
i see *you*, hard to look at, on all sides with irradiance of fire, blazing sun—immeasurable.

18

you, the imperishable, the supreme, to be known;*
you are the universe's ultimate basis;
you, the changeless guardian of everlasting dharma;
the eternal purusha, you, i believe.

19

without beginning, middle, end; of infinite power;
endless armed; the sun, moon, your eyes,
i see you, blazing fire your faces, with your refulgence this universe searing.

20

this space between heaven and earth, surely, is pervaded by just you, and the dishas all;**
seeing this your astounding, dreadful form, the three worlds are terrified, mahatman.

---

*the thing to be known.

**the four quarters, directions of the sky.

21

amī hi tvāṁ surasaṁghā viśanti
kecid bhītāḥ prāñjalayo gṛṇanti
svastī 'ty uktvā maharṣisiddhasaṁghāḥ
stuvanti tvāṁ stutibhiḥ puṣkalābhiḥ

22

rudrādityā vasavo ye ca sādhyā
viśve 'śvinau marutaś co 'ṣmapāś ca
gandharvayakṣāsurasiddhasaṁghā
vīkṣante tvāṁ vismitāś cai 'va sarve

23

rūpaṁ mahat te bahuvaktranetraṁ
mahābāho bahubāhūrupādam
bahūdaraṁ bahudaṁṣṭrākarālaṁ
dṛṣṭvā lokāḥ pravyathitās tathā 'ham

24

nabhaḥspṛśaṁ dīptam anekavarṇaṁ
vyāttānanaṁ dīptaviśālanetram
dṛṣṭvā hi tvāṁ pravyathitāntarātmā
dhṛtiṁ na vindāmi śamaṁ ca viṣṇo

25

daṁṣṭrākarālāni ca te mukhāni
dṛṣṭvai 'va kālānalasaṁnibhāni
diśo na jāne na labhe ca śarma
prasīda deveśa jagannivāsa

21

ah, *you* these hosts of suras enter; some, in fear, hands folded, give praise;
svasti!,† so crying, the maharishi, siddha hosts adore *you* with hymns of fervent praise.

22

the rudras, adityas, vasus, and these sadhyas; the viswas, the two asvins and the maruts, and the usmapas;*
the gandharvas, the yakshas, the asuras, siddha hosts gaze at you in wonder, also, surely, all.

23

your great *form*, many-mouthed, -eyed, mahabaho, of many arms, thighs, feet,
many bellies, many fangs, horrible, seeing, the worlds tremble, as also i.

24

sky-touching, ablaze, countless-hued, mouth agape, huge blazing eyes:
seeing only *you*, my inmost soul quails; no stability do i find, nor peace, o vishnu.

25

and seeing your fearful, fanged mouths, like time's fire flaming,
the directions i do not know, nor find joy—be merciful, lord of gods, abode of the universe!

---

†hail, peace!
*manes, ancestors.

26

amī ca tvāṁ dhṛtarāṣṭrasya putrāḥ
sarve sahai 'vā 'vanipālasaṁghaih
bhīṣmo droṇaḥ sūtaputras thatā 'sau
sahā 'smadīyair api yodhamukhyaiḥ

27

vaktrāṇi te tvaramāṇā viśanti
daṁṣṭrākarālāni bhayānakāni
kecid vilagnā daśanāntareṣu
saṁdṛśyant cūrṇitair uttamāṅgaiḥ

28

yathā nadīnāṁ bahavo 'mbuvegāḥ
samudram evā 'bhimukhā dravanti
tathā tavā 'mī naralokavīrā
viśanti vaktrāṇy abhivijvalanti

29

yathā pradīptaṁ jvalanaṁ pataṅgā
viśanti nāśāya samṛddhavegāḥ
thatai 'va nāśāya viśanti lokās
tavā 'pi vaktrāṇi samṛddhavegāḥ

30

lelihyase grasamānaḥ samantāl
lokān samagrān vadanair jvaladbhiḥ
tejobhir āpūrya jagat samagraṁ
bhāsas tavo 'grāḥ pratapanti viṣṇo

26

and dhritarashtra's sons, all, with the hosts of kings;
bheeshma, drona, and that sutaputra,* also, with our side's main warriors, too,

27

into your fearful jaws, terrible with fangs, rush;
some stick between the teeth: are seen, heads crushed.

28

as many rivers' swift waters just towards the ocean flow,
even so, those heroes of the world of men enter your blazing mouths.

29

as a burning fire moths enter, to perish swiftly,
even so, to perish, these men, also, fly into your mouths at great speed.

30

you lick,** devouring on all sides the worlds, entirely, with mouths aflame;
your brilliance covers all the universe, your lustre terrible, searing, o vishnu.

---

*karna.

**them up, while.

31

ākhyāhi me ko bhavān ugrarūpo
namo 'stu te devavara prasīda
vijñātum icchāmi bhavantam ādyaṁ
na hi prajānāmi tava pravṛittim

32

śrībhagavān uvāca
kālo 'smi lokakṣayakṛt pravṛddho
lokān samāhartum iha pravṛttaḥ
ṛte 'pi tvāṁ na bhaviṣyanti sarve
ye 'vasthitāḥ pratyanīkeṣu yodhāḥ

33

tasmāt tvam uttiṣṭha yaśo labhasva
jitvā śatrūn bhuṅkṣva rājyaṁ samṛddham
mayai 'vai 'e nihatāḥ pūrvam eva
nimittamātraṁ bhava savyasācin

34

droṇaṁ ca bhīṣmaṁ ca jayadrathaṁ ca
karṇaṁ tathā 'nyān api yodhavīrān
mayā hatāṁs tvaṁ jahi mā vyathiṣṭhā
yudhyasva jetāsi raṇe sapatnān

35

saṁjaya uvāca
etac chrutvā vacanaṁ keśavasya
kṛtāñjalir vepamānaḥ kirīṭī
namaskṛtvā bhūya evā 'ha kṛṣṇaṁ
sagadgadaṁ bhītabhītaḥ praṇamya

31

tell me who *you* are, of dreadful form;
salutations to *you,* best of gods, have mercy!
i want to know *you,* the *first,*
for i do not understand what *you* do.

32

the gracious lord said:
time i am, world-waster, ancient—the world to annihilate, here, my mission;
even without you,* no future have all these, arrayed hostile, the warriors.

33

so, arise, glory gain: defeating your enemies, enjoy a thriving kingdom;
by me alone these have been killed already—the instrument, only, become, savyasachin.†

34

drona and bheeshma and jayadratha and karna, as also other warrior heroes, by me slain already, you raze; do not be afraid —fight, you will conquer in battle, the enemies.

35

sanjaya said:
hearing these words of kesava, hands folded, trembling, kiriti**
bowed, again, spoke to krishna, falteringly, in terror, prostrating.

---

*killing them.
†arjuna was ambidextrous.
**arjuna, the crown-wearer.

36

arjuna uvāca

sthāne hṛṣīkeśa tava prakīrtyā
jagat prahṛṣyaty anurajyate ca
rakṣāṁsi bhītāni diśo dravanti
sarve namasyanti ca siddhasaṁghāḥ

37

kasmāc ca te na nameran mahātman
garīyase brahmaṇo 'py ādikartre
ananta deveśa jagannivāsa
tvam akṣaraṁ sad asat tatparaṁ yat

38

tvam ādidevaḥ puruṣaḥ purāṇas
tvam asya viśvasya paraṁ nidhānam
vettā si vedyaṁ ca paraṁ ca dhāma
tvayā tataṁ viśvam anantarūpa

39

vāyur yamo 'gnir varuṇaḥ śaśāṅkaḥ
prajāpatis tvaṁ prapitāmahaś ca
namo namas te 'stu sahasrakṛtvaḥ
punaś ca bhūyo 'pi namo namas te

40

namaḥ purastād atha pṛṣṭhatas te
namo 'stu te sarvata eva sarva
anantavīryāmitavikramas tvaṁ
sarvaṁ samāpnoṣi tato 'si sarvaḥ

36

arjuna said:
rightly, hrishikesa, by your praises is the world enraptured and fascinated;
raskhasas, terrified, flee in all directions, and the siddha hosts pay homage.

37

and why not worship *you*, mahataman, who are greater than brahma even, the first creator;
o infinite, lord of gods, abode of the universe, you are deathless; real, unreal; and *what* is beyond that.

38

you, the first god, the ancient purusha; *you* are the supreme home of the universe;
you are the knower and the known* and the final resort—by *you* the universe is pervaded, infinite-formed!

39

vayu, yama, agni, varuna, sashanka, and prajapati,† the great grandsire—*you*.
hail, hail to *you*, a thousand times, and again, yet again, hail, hail to *you*!

40

obeisance in front, also from behind, to *you*; obeisance to *you* on every side, o *all*!
of endless prowess, boundless compass, *you*; everything, *you* suffuse, so *you* are all.

---

*knowable, that which is to be known.
†the gods wind, death, fire, sea, moon, brahma.

41

sakhe 'ti matvā prasabhaṁ yad uktaṁ
he kṛṣṇa he yādava he sakhe 'ti
ajānatā mahimānaṁ tave 'daṁ
mayā pramādāt praṇayena vā 'pi

42

yac cā 'vahāsārtham asatkṛto 'si
vihāraśayyāsanabhojaneṣu
eko 'thavā 'py acyuta tatsamakṣaṁ
tat kṣāmaye tvām aham aprameyam

43

pitā 'si lokasya carācarasya
tvam asya pūjyaś ca gurur garīyān
na tvatsamo 'sty abhyadhikaḥ kuto 'nyo
lokatraye 'py apratimaprabhāva

44

tasmāt praṇamya praṇidhāya kāyaṁ
prasādaye tvām aham īśam īḍyam
pite 'va putrasya sakhe 'va sakhyuḥ
priyaḥ priyāyā 'rhasi deva soḍhum

45

adṛṣṭapūrvaṁ hṛṣito 'smi dṛṣṭvā
bhayena ca pravyathitaṁ mano me
tad eva me darśaya deva rūpaṁ
prasīda deveśa jagannivāsa

41

'my friend', so thinking, rashly, whatever i said, 'o krishna', 'o yadava', 'o friend', thus,
not knowing this your greatness, out of my carelessness or out of love,

42

and whatever slight, in jest, was shown, at sport, lying down, seated, while eating,
alone or, achyuta, in the presence of others—all that forgive me, o incomprehensible.

43

the father you are of this world, of the moving, the unmoving; you are its adored and loftiest guru;
none is your equal, how then any greater, in the three worlds, as well, o unequalled power?

44

so, bowing, prostrating my body, i worship you, lord adorable;
as a father his son, a friend his friend, a lover his beloved, you must, lord, suffer me.

45

the never-before-seen, seeing, i rejoice, and with fear my heart is shaken so;
so, lord, your other form show me—be merciful, god of gods, home of the universe!

46

kirīṭinaṁ gadinaṁ cakrahastam
icchāmi tvāṁ draṣṭum ahaṁ tathai 'va
tenai 'va rūpeṇa caturbhujena
sahasrabāho bhava viśvamūrte

47

śrībhagavan uvāca
mayā prasannena tavā 'rjune 'daṁ
rūpaṁ paraṁ darśitam ātmayogāt
tejomayaṁ viśvam anantam ādyaṁ
yan me tvadanyena na dṛṣṭapūrvam

48

na vedayajñādhyayanair na dānair
na ca kriyābhir na tapobhir ugraiḥ
evaṁrūpaḥ śakya ahaṁ nṛloke
draṣṭuṁ tvadanyena kurupravīra

49

mā te vyathā mā ca vimūḍhabhāvo
dṛṣṭvā rūpaṁ ghoram īdṛṅ mame 'dam
vyapetabhīḥ prītamanāḥ punas tvaṁ
tad eva me rūpam idaṁ prapaśya

50

saṁjaya uvāca
ity arjunaṁ vāsudevas thato 'ktvā
svakaṁ rūpaṁ darśayām āsa bhūyaḥ
āśvāsayām āsa ca bhītam enaṁ
bhūtvā punaḥ saumyavapur mahātmā

46
crowned, with mace, disc in your hands—i want to see you, just as before;
that same form, four-armed, assume, o thousand-armed, universe-bodied!

47
the gracious lord said:
by my grace, to you, arjuna, this form supreme was shown, through my divine yoga—
resplendent, universal, infinite, primal, which none but you has seen before.

48
not by the veda, sacrifice, learning, not by charity, and not by rituals, not by fierce penance,
in this form can i, in the world of men, be seen by anyone but you, o kurupravira.*

49
do not be afraid, nor confounded, seeing this terrible *form*, like this, of mine;
free from fear, with a glad heart, again, then, the same, this my form, see.

50
sanjaya said:
thus to arjuna saying, vaasudeva his own form showed again,
and comforted that terrified, becoming once more the gentle, beautiful mahatman.

---

*great hero of the kurus.

51

arjuna uvāca
dṛṣṭve 'daṁ mānuṣaṁ rūpaṁ
tava saumyaṁ janārdana
idānīm asmi saṁvṛttaḥ
sacetāḥ prakṛtiṁ gataḥ

52

śrībhagavān uvāca
sudurdarśam idaṁ rūpaṁ
dṛṣṭavān asi yan mama
devā apy asya rūpasya
nityaṁ darśanakāṅkṣiṇaḥ

53

nā 'haṁ vedair na tapasā
na dānena na ce 'jyayā
śakya evaṁvidho draṣṭuṁ
dṛṣṭavān asi māṁ yathā

54

bhaktyā tv ananyayā śakya
aham evaṁvidho 'rjuna
jñātuṁ draṣṭuṁ ca tattvena
praveṣṭuṁ ca paraṁtapa

55

matkarmakṛn matparamo
madbhaktaḥ saṅgavarjitaḥ
nirvairaḥ sarvabhūteṣu
yaḥ sa mām eti pāṇḍava

51

arjuna said:

seeing this human form of yours, gracious, janardana,
now, i become calm, return to myself.

52

the gracious lord said:

most difficult to see, this *form* which you have seen, of mine;
the devas, even, always, this form to see are keen.

53

not through the veda, not by tapasya, not through daana, nor yet by yagnas,
can i like this be seen, as you have seen me.

54

but through devotion, singular, can i like this, arjuna,
be known, seen, and, in truth, also entered into, parantapa.

55

who for me does work; i his supreme; my devotee, of attachment rid;
without hostility towards any of the living, he comes to me, pandava.

this is the eleventh canto of the srimad bhagavad gita named viswarupa darshana yoga

canto 12

the way of devotion

1

arjuna uvāca
evaṁ satatayuktā ye
bhaktās tvāṁ paryupāsate
ye cā 'py akṣaram avyaktaṁ
teṣāṁ ke yogavittamāḥ

2

śrībhagavān uvāca
mayy āveśya mano ye māṁ
nityayuktā upāsate
śraddhayā parayo 'petās
te me yuktatamā matāḥ

3

ye tv akṣaram anirdeśyam
avyaktaṁ paryupāsate
sarvatragam acintyaṁ ca
kūṭastham acalaṁ dhruvam

4

saṁniyamye 'ndriyagrāmaṁ
sarvatra samabuddhayaḥ
te prāpnuvanti mām eva
sarvabhūtahite ratāḥ

5

kleśo 'dhikataras teṣām
avyaktāsaktacetasām
avyaktā hi gatir duḥkhaṁ
dehavadbhir avāpyate

1

arjuna said:
thus, always yoked, those devotees who worship you,
and, again, those who do the imperishable, the
unmanifest—of these, which have yoga?

2

the gracious lord said:
on me fixing the mind, who, ever absorbed, me worship,
with devotion supreme endowed, them, i, the best yogis
consider.

3

but who the imperishable, ineffable,
unmanifest, worship,
the ubiquitous and inconceivable,
highest, unmoving, permanent,

4

restraining all the senses, everywhere even-minded,
they attain me, surely—to the weal of all beings devoted.

5

the travail greater of them, on the unmanifest whose
minds are set;
for, the way of the unmanifest is painfully by the
embodied attained.

6

ye tu sarvāṇi karmāṇi
mayi saṁnyasya matparāḥ
ananyenai 'va yogena
māṁ dhyāyanta upāsate

7

teṣāṃ ahaṁ samuddhartā
mṛtyusaṁsārasāgarāt
bhavāmi nacirāt pārtha
mayy āveśitacetasām

8

mayy eva mana ādhatsva
mayi buddhiṁ niveśaya
nivasiṣyasi mayy eva
ata ūrdhvaṁ na saṁśayaḥ

9

atha cittaṁ samādhātuṁ
na śaknoṣi mayi sthiram
abhyāsayogena tato
māṁ icchā 'ptuṁ dhanaṁjaya

10

abhyāse 'py asamartho 'si
matkarmaparamo bhava
madartham api karmāṇi
kurvan siddhim avāpsyasi

6

but who all karma to me renounce, on me intent,
with singular yoga, me, through meditation, worship:

7

of them, i, the deliverer from death, samsara's* sea,
become, quickly, partha—on me whose minds are set.

8

on me alone your heart set; in me let your mind dwell:
you will live in me, surely, thereafter, beyond doubt.

9

if your mind you cannot fix on me, steadily,
through the practice of yoga, then, me seek to attain,
dhananjaya.

10

practice,** even, if you cannot do, let my work your highest be;
for my sake, even, work doing, perfection you will find.

*the mortal world of delusion, transmigration.
**the exercise of yoga.

11

athai 'tad apy aśakto 'si
kartuṁ madyogam āśritaḥ
sarvakarmaphalatyāgaṁ
'ataḥ kuru yatātmavān

12

śreyo hi jñānam abhyāsāj
jñānād dhyānaṁ viśiṣyate
dhyānāt karmaphalatyāgas
tyāgāc chāntir anantaram

13

adveṣṭā sarvabhūtānāṁ
maitraḥ karuṇa eva ca
nirmamo nirahaṁkāraḥ
samaduḥkhasukhaḥ kṣamī

14

saṁtuṣṭaḥ satataṁ yogī
yatātmā dṛḍhaniścayaḥ
mayy arpitamanobuddhir
yo madbhaktaḥ sa me priyaḥ

15

yasmān no 'dvijate loko
lokān no 'dvijate ca yaḥ
harṣāmarṣabhayodvegair
mukto yaḥ sa ca me priyaḥ

11

if even this you cannot do, in performing yoga for me refuge;
all karma's fruit renounce, then, with subdued mind.

12

better, surely, knowledge than routine; than knowledge meditation is superior;
than meditation, the sacrifice of karma's fruit—upon renunciation, peace follows.

13

without aversion towards any creature;
friendly and compassionate only;
without 'mine', without 'i';
equal in pain, pleasure; forgiving;

14

contended always, the yogi;
self-controlled, of firm resolve;
to me given heart, mind—who is my devotee,
he is dear to me.

15

by whom the world is not disturbed; and the world does not disturb him;
from exultation, anger, fear, agitation who is free, he, too, is dear to me.

16

anapekṣaḥ śucir dakṣa
udāsīno gatavyathaḥ
sarvārambhaparityāgī
yo madbhaktaḥ sa me priyaḥ

17

yo na hṛṣyati na dveṣṭi
na śocati na kāṅkṣati
śubhāśubhaparityāgī
bhaktimān yaḥ sa me priyaḥ

18

samaḥ śatrau ca mitre ca
tathā mānāpamānayoḥ
śītoṣṇasukhaduḥkheṣu
amaḥ saṅgavivarjitaḥ

19

tulyanindāstutir mauni
saṁtuṣṭo yena kenacit
aniketaḥ sthiramatir
bhaktimān me priyo naraḥ

20

ye tu dharmyāmṛtam idaṁ
yathoktaṁ paryupāsate
śraddhadhānā matparamā
bhaktās te 'tīva me priyāḥ

16

independent, pure, competent, indifferent, free from pain;
who all endeavour has abandoned—
my devotee, he is dear to me.

17

who neither exults nor dislikes;
neither grieves nor desires;
good, evil, abandons—that devotee, he is dear to me.

18

and alike with enemy and friend;
also, to honour, dishonour;
in heat, cold, joy, sorrow, the same;
free from attachment;

19

equal in blame, praise; quiet, contented with anything;*
homeless, of firm resolve—my devotee, a man dear to me.

20

but who this immortal dharma, as told, follow,
with faith, me the† goal, those devotees are very dear to me.

this is the twelfth canto of the srimad bhagavad gita named the bhakti yoga

---

*which comes.
†their.

canto 13

the way of discernment between

the field and its knower

arjuna uvāca
prakṛtiṁ puruṣaṁ caiva
ksetraṁ ksetrajñam eva ca
etad veditum icchāmi
jñānaṁ jñeyaṁ ca keśava

1
śrībhagavān uvāca
idaṁ śarīraṁ kaunteya
kṣetram ity abhidhīyate
etad yo vetti taṁ prāhuḥ
kṣetrajña iti tadvidaḥ

2
kṣetrajñaṁ cā 'pi māṁ viddhi
sarvakṣetreṣu bhārata
kṣetrakṣetrajñayor jñānaṁ
yat taj jñānaṁ mataṁ mama

3
tat kṣetraṁ yac ca yādṛk ca
yadvikāri yataś ca yat
sa ca yo yatprabhāvaś ca
tat samāsena me śṛṇu

arjuna said:*
prakriti and purusha, also; kshetra and kshetrajna, too:
these, i wish to know; knowledge and the known, kesava.

1
the gracious lord said:
this body, kaunteya, the field it is called;
this who knows, he is called kshetrajna,† by those who know.

2
and the kshetrajna, also, me, in every field, bhaarata;
of kshetra, kshetrajna,‡ the knowledge:
that, true knowledge, in my view.

3
and what that field is, and what its nature, and what its transformations, whence arisen,
and what *he*** is, and of what origin—
that, in brief, from me hear.

---

*this verse is not included in many versions. if it is, the number of slokas in the bhagavad gita becomes 701, instead of 700. as in radhakrishnan's translation, i have not numbered it here.

†knower of the field.

‡swami vireswarananda: matter and spirit

**the kshetrajna.

4

ṛṣibhir bahudhā gītaṁ
chandobhir vividhaiḥ pṛthak
brahmasūtrapadaiś cai 'va
hetumadbhir viniścitaiḥ

5

mahābhūtāny ahaṁkāro
buddhir avyaktam eva ca
indriyāṇi daśai 'kaṁ ca
pañca ce ndriyagocarāḥ

6

icchā dveṣaḥ sukhaṁ duḥkhaṁ
saṁghātaś cetanā dhṛtiḥ
etat kṣetraṁ samāsena
savikāram udāhṛtam

7

amānitvam adambhitvam
ahiṁsā kṣāntir ārjavam
ācāryopāsanaṁ śaucaṁ
sthairyam ātmavinigrahaḥ

8

indriyārtheṣu vairāgyam
anahaṁkāra eva ca
anmamṛtyujarāvyādhi-
duḥkhadoṣānudarśanam

4

by the rishis, variously, sung, in chhandas,† diversely, distinctly;
and also in brahma sutra‡ passages, logical, decisive.

5

the mahabhutas,** ego, intelligence, and also the unmanifest;
the senses, ten, and the one,*** and five sense pastures;

6

desire, aversion; pleasure, pain; the organism, consciousness, fortitude—
thus, the field, in brief, is described, with examples.

7

humility, integrity, non-violence, patience, uprightness;
serving the guru, purity, stability, self-control;

8

for the objects of sensuality, aversion;
lack of egotism; and also,
in birth, death, old age, sickness—pain, evil, seeing;

---

†vedic hymns.
‡aphorisms of brahman.
**the five elements.
***mind.

9

asaktir anabhiṣvaṅgaḥ
putradāragṛhādiṣu
nityaṁ ca samacittatvam
iṣṭāniṣṭopapattiṣu

10.

mayi cā 'nanyayogena
bhaktir avyabhicāriṇī
viviktadeśasevitvam
aratir janasaṁsadi

11

adhyātmajñānanityatvaṁ
tattvajñānārthadarśanam
etaj jñānam iti proktam
ajñānaṁ yad ato 'nyathā

12

jñeyaṁ yat tat pravakṣyāmi
yaj jñātvā 'mṛtam aśnute
anādimat paraṁ brahma
na sat tan nā 'sad ucyate

13

sarvataḥpāṇipādaṁ tat
sarvatokṣiśiromukham
sarvataḥśrutimal loke
sarvam āvṛtya tiṣṭhati

9

detachment, no clinging to son, wife, home, the likes;
and, always, even-mindedness to desired,* unwanted happenings;

10

and for me, through exclusive yoga, devotion abiding;
to solitary places resorting; distaste for gatherings of men;

11

in spiritual wisdom, constancy; the knowledge of truth's end seeing—
all this gyana is called; ignorance, what is other than this.

12

that which is known, i will tell you, which knowing immortality is gained;
beginningless, it, supreme brahman; neither being, that, nor unbeing, it is told.

13

everywhere, hands, feet: that; everywhere, eyes, heads, faces;
everywhere, ears—in the world everything enveloping, it dwells.

---

*and.

14

sarvendriyaguṇābhāsaṁ
sarvendriyavivarjitam
asaktaṁ sarvabhṛc cai 'va
nirguṇaṁ guṇabhoktṛ ca

15

bahir antas ca bhūtānām
acaraṁ caram eva ca
sūkṣmatvāt tad avijñeyaṁ
dūrasthaṁ cā 'ntike ca tat

16

avibhaktaṁ ca bhūteṣu
vibhaktam iva ca sthitam
bhūtabhartṛ ca taj jñeyaṁ
grasiṣṇu prabhaviṣṇu ca

17

jyotiṣām api taj jyotis
tamasaḥ param ucyate
jñānaṁ jñeyaṁ jñānagamyaṁ
hṛdi sarvasya dhiṣṭhitam

18

iti kṣetraṁ tathā jñānaṁ
jñeyaṁ co 'ktaṁ samāsataḥ
madbhakta etad vijñāya
madbhāvāyo 'papadyate

14
all the senses' qualities reflecting, of all the senses devoid;
unattached and also all-supporting; without gunas and experiencing the gunas.

15
outside and within the living, mobile and unmoving, too;
being subtle, that, imperceptible; and far and near, that.

16
and undivided, in beings, also, seemingly, divided, exists;
and as beings' support that is known, devourer and creator.

17
of lights, also, that the light, beyond darkness, said to be;
knowledge, the known, gained through knowledge, in the hearts of all seated.

18
thus, the field and also knowledge and the known, told in brief;
my devotee, this knowing, to my being attains.

19

prakṛtiṁ puruṣaṁ cai 'va
viddhy anādī ubhāv api
vikārāṁś ca guṇāṁś cai 'va
viddhi prakṛtisaṁbhavān

20

kārya karaṇa kartṛtve
hetuḥ prakṛtir ucyate
puruṣaḥ sukhaduḥkhānāṁ
bhoktṛtve hetur ucyate

21

puruṣaḥ prakṛtistho hi
bhuṅkte prakṛtijān guṇān
kāraṇaṁ guṇasaṅgo 'sya
sadasadyonijanmasu

22

upadraṣṭā 'numantā ca
bhartā bhoktā maheśvaraḥ
paramātme 'ti cā 'py ukto
dehe 'smin puruṣaḥ paraḥ

23

ya evaṁ vetti puruṣaṁ
prakṛtiṁ ca guṇaiḥ saha
sarvathā vartamāno 'pi
na sa bhūyo 'bhijāyate

19

prakriti* and also purusha,† know, are beginningless, both;
and transformations and also gunas, know—of prakriti born.

20

effect, cause, instrument, agency—prakriti, it is told;
purusha, of joy, sorrow, experience, the cause, it's said.

21

for, the purusha, dwelling in prakriti, enjoys the prakriti-born gunas;
the cause, attachment to the gunas: of its birth in good, evil wombs.

22

witness and sanctioner, lord, experiencer, great *god,*
and also the supreme soul, it's told—in this body, the purusha transcendent.

23

who thus knows purusha and prakriti, with the gunas,
whatever his life, he is not born again.

---

*nature, the feminine principle.
†soul, the masculine principle.

24

dhyānenā 'tmani paśyanti
kecid ātmānam ātmanā
anye sāṁkhyena yogena
karmayogena cā 'pare

25

anye tv evam ajānantaḥ
śrutvā 'nyebhya upāsate
te 'pi cā 'titaranty eva
mṛtyuṁ śrutiparāyaṇaḥ

26

yāvat saṁjāyate kiṁcit
sattvaṁ sthāvarajaṅgamam
kṣetrakṣetrajñasaṁyogāt
tad viddhi bharatarṣabha

27

samaṁ sarveṣu bhūteṣu
tiṣṭhantaṁ parameśvaram
vinaśyatsv avinaśyantaṁ
yaḥ paśyati sa paśyati

28

samaṁ paśyan hi sarvatra
samavasthitam īśvaram
na hinasty ātmanā 'tmānaṁ
tato yāti parāṁ gatim

24

through meditation, the atman see, some, in the atman with the atman;

others, through samkhya yoga, and by karma yoga, others.

25

yet others, not thus knowing, hearing from others, worship;

and they also, surely, transcend death by devotion to what they hear.*

26

whatever being is born, motionless or mobile—

from kshetra and kshetrajna's union: that know, bharatarishabha.

27

equally in all creatures abiding, the supreme *god*,

amidst the perishing, imperishable, who sees, he sees.

28

for, the same *god* seeing, everywhere, omnipresent,

he injures not the atman with the atman, so attains the final goal.

---

*sruti is also the veda.

29

prakṛtyai 'va ca karmāṇi
kriyamāṇāni sarvaśaḥ
yaḥ paśyati thatā 'tmānam
akartāraṁ sa paśyati

30

yadā bhūtapṛthagbhāvam
ekastham anupaśyati
tata eva ca vistāraṁ
brahma saṁpadyate tadā

31

anāditvān nirguṇatvāt
paramātmā 'yam avyayaḥ
śarīrastho 'pi kaunteya
Na karoti na lipyate

32

yathā sarvagataṁ saukṣmyād
ākāśaṁ no 'palipyate
sarvatrā 'vasthito dehe
tathā 'tmā no 'palipyate

33

yathā prakāśayaty ekaḥ
kṛtsnaṁ lokam imaṁ raviḥ
kṣetraṁ kṣetrī tathā kṛtsnaṁ
prakāśayati bhārata

29

and only by prakriti, karma is done, in every way,
who sees, also that the atman is actless, he sees.

30

when the diversity of beings as situated in the *one*, he sees,
and also, therefrom, their spread, the brahman he then becomes.

31

beginningless, without attributes, this paramatma, immortal,
though dwelling in the body, kaunteya, neither acts nor is tainted.

32

as, being subtle, the ubiquitous ether is not tainted,
so also, everywhere located, in the body, the atman is not stained.

33

as one sun illumines this whole world,
so, too, the kshetri* illumines this entire kshetra,† bhaarata.

---

*embodied soul.
†field, universe.

34

kṣetrakṣetrajñayor evam
antaraṁ jñānacakṣuṣā
bhūtaprakṛtimokṣaṁ ca
ye vidur yānti te param

34
between kshetra, kshetrajna, thus,
the distinction, with eye of wisdom,
and the deliverance of beings from prakriti,
who know, they attain the supreme.

this is the thirteenth canto of the srimad bhagavad gita named kshetra kshetrajna vibhaga yoga

canto 14

the way of the division of the three gunas

1

śrībhagavān uvāca
paraṁ bhūyaḥ pravakṣyāmi
jñānānāṁ jñānam uttamam
yaj jñātvā munayaḥ sarve
parāṁ siddhim ito gatāḥ

2

idaṁ jñānam upāśritya
mama sādharmyam āgatāḥ
sarge 'pi no 'paj āyante
pralaye na vyathanti ca

3

mama yonir mahad brahma
tasmin garbhaṁ dadhāmy aham
saṁbhavaḥ sarvabhūtānāṁ
tato bhavati bhārata

4

sarvayonisu kaunteya
mūrtayaḥ saṁbhavanti yāḥ
tāsāṁ brahma mahad yonir
aham bījapradaḥ pitā

5

sattvaṁ rajas tama iti
guṇāḥ prakṛtisaṁbhavāḥ
nibadhnanti mahābāho
dehe dehinam avyayam

1

the gracious lord said:
again, the highest i will tell you, of wisdoms the best wisdom;
this knowing, the sages, all, to final perfection from here passed.

2

to this wisdom resorting, my nature attaining,
at creation, even, they are not born, and not during the dissolution disquieted.

3

my womb great brahma, into which the seed cast i;
to birth all beings, from that, come, bhaarata.

4

in all the species, kaunteya, whatever forms take birth,
of them, great brahma the womb, i the seed-giving father.

5

sattva, rajas, tamas, these gunas, prakriti-born,
bind, mahabaho, into the body the dweller imperishable.

6

tatra sattvaṁ nirmalatvāt
prakāśakam anāmayam
sukhasaṅgena badhnāti
jñānasaṅgena cā 'nagha

7

rajo rāgātmakaṁ viddhi
tṛṣṇāsaṅgasamudbhavam
tan nibadhnāti kaunteya
karmasaṅgena dehinam

8

tamas tv ajñānajaṁ viddhi
mohanaṁ sarvadehinām
pramādālasyanidrābhis
tan nibadhnāti bhārata

9

sattvaṁ sukhe sañjayati
rajaḥ karmaṇi bhārata
jñānam āvṛtya tu tamaḥ
pramāde sañjayaty uta

10

rajas tamaś cā 'bhibhūya
sattvaṁ bhavati bhārata
rajaḥ sattvaṁ tamaś cai 'va
tamaḥ sattvaṁ rajas tathā

6

of these, sattva, being pure, is illumining, health-giving, through attachment to happiness binds, and through attachment to knowledge, o sinless.

7

rajas has passion's nature, know, from craving, attachment, sprung;
it binds, kaunteya, with addiction to action, the embodied.

8

but tamas, ignorance-born, know, deludes all the living; through rashness, sloth, stupor, it binds fast, bhaarata.

9

sattva to happiness binds; rajas to activity, bhaarata; but, wisdom shrouding, tamas to rashness, it's told.

10

rajas and tamas subduing, sattva prevails, bhaarata; rajas, the same, over sattva and tamas; tamas, even so, over sattva and rajas.

11

sarvadvāreṣu dehe 'smin
prakāśa upajāyate
jñānaṁ yadā tadā vidyād
vivṛddhaṁ sattvam ity uta

12

lobhaḥ pravṛttir ārambhaḥ
karmaṇām aśamaḥ spṛhā
rajasy etāni jāyante
vivṛddhe bharatarṣabha

13

aprakāśo 'pravṛttiś ca
pramādo moha eva ca
tamasy etāni jāyante
vivṛddhe kurunandana

14

yadā sattve pravṛddhe tu
pralayaṁ yāti dehabhṛt
tado 'ttamavidāṁ lokān
amalān pratipadyate

15

rajasi pralayaṁ gatvā
karmasaṅgiṣu jāyate
tathā pralīnas tamasi
mūḍhayoniṣu jāyate

11

when through all doors* of this body, light radiates,
knowledge—then, know, sattva surely waxes.

12

greed, activity, undertaking karma, disquiet, desire—
when rajas increases, these prevail, bharatarishabha.

13

darkness and inactivity, neglect and also delusion:
when tamas increases, these prevail, joy of the kurus.

14

now, while sattva waxes, if to dissolution** the embodied goes,
then, worlds of the highest sages, taintless, it gains.

15

in rajas, death finding, among those addicted to karma, it is born;
and if dissolved during tamas, in dark wombs it is born.

---

*of perception.
**death.

16

karmaṇaḥ sukṛtasyā 'huḥ
sāttvikaṁ nirmalaṁ phalam
rajasas tu phalaṁ duḥkham
ajñānaṁ tamasaḥ phalam

17

sattvāt saṁjāyate jñānaṁ
rajaso lobha eva ca
pramādamohau tamaso
bhavato 'jñānam eva ca

18

ūrdhvaṁ gacchanti sattvasthā
madhye tiṣṭhanti rājasāḥ
jaghanyaguṇavṛttisthā
adho gacchanti tāmasāḥ

19

nā 'nyaṁ guṇebhyaḥ kartāraṁ
yadā draṣṭā 'nupaśyati
guṇebhyaś ca paraṁ vetti
madbhāvaṁ so 'dhigacchati

20

guṇān etān atītya trīn
dehī dehasamudbhavān
janmamṛtyujarāduḥkhair
vimukto 'mṛtam aśnute

16
of virtuous karma, it is told, sattvik and pure the fruit;
while rajas' fruit is sorrow, and darkness the fruit of tamas.

17
from sattva arises knowledge; and from rajas only greed;
heedlessness, delusion, from tamas come, and also ignorance.

18
upwards go those founded in sattva;
midway remain the rajasas;
those steeped in the vile guna, go downwards, the tamasas.

19
no other agent than the gunas, when the seer sees,
and what is beyond the gunas knows, to my being he attains.

20
these gunas transcending, three, which spring from the body, the embodied,
from birth, death, old age, pain, is liberated, immortality gains.

21

arjuna uvāca

kair liṅgais trīn guṇān etān
atīto bhavati prabho
kimācāraḥ kathaṁ cai 'tāṁs
trīn guṇān ativartate

22

śrībhagavān uvāca

prakāśṁ ca pravṛttiṁ ca
moham eva ca pāṇḍava
na dveṣṭi saṁpravṛttāni
na nivṛttāni kāṅkṣati

23

udāsīnavad āsīno
guṇair yo na vicālyate
guṇā vartanta ity eva
yo 'vatiṣṭhati ne 'ṅgate

24

samaduḥkhasukhaḥ svasthaḥ
samaloṣṭāśmakāñcanaḥ
tulyapriyāpriyo dhīras
tulyanindātmasaṁstutiḥ

25

mānāpamānayos tulyas
tulyo mitrāripakṣayoḥ
sarvārambhaparityāgī
guṇātītaḥ sa ucyate

21

arjuna said:

what signs of one who these three gunas has transcended, lord?
what his deportment, and how does he the three gunas transcend?

22

the gracious lord said:

light and activity and, even, delusion,
pandava, he does not shun, when they arise, nor, when they cease, long for.

23

as if indifferent seated, by the gunas who is not moved;
the gunas act: this knowing, who is still, unwavering.

24

the same in joy, sorrow, contented; equal* a clod, stone, gold;
the same to the pleasant, unpleasant; calm; equal to blame of himself, to praise.

25

in honour, disgrace, the same; equal to a friend, an enemy; all endeavours who has renounced—gone beyond the gunas, he is said to have.

*for him.

26

māṁ ca yo 'vyabhicāreṇa
bhaktiyogena sevate
sa guṇān samatītyai 'tān
brahmabhūyāya kalpate

27

brahmaṇo hi pratiṣṭhā 'ham
amṛtasyā 'vyayasya ca
śāśvatasya ca dharmasya
sukhasyai 'kāntikasya ca

26

and me who, with unfailing yoga of devotion, serves,
he, these gunas transcends, for becoming brahman is
fit.

27

for, brahman's abode, *i*, immortal and imperishable;
and of eternal dharma, and absolute bliss.

this is the fourteenth canto of the srimad bhagavad gita named gunatrai vibhaga yoga

canto 15

the way of the supreme person

1

ūrdhvamūlam adhaḥśākham
aśvatthaṁ prāhur avyayam
chandāṁsi yasya parṇāni
yas taṁ veda sa vedavit

2

adhaś co 'radhvaṁ prasṛtās tasya śākhā
guṇapravṛddhā viṣayapravālāḥ
adhaś ca mūlāny anusaṁtatāni
karmānubandhīni manuṣyaloke

3

na rūpam asye 'ha tatho 'palabhyate
nā 'nto na cā 'dir na ca saṁpratiṣṭhā
aśvattham enaṁ suvirūḍhamūlam
asaṅgaśastreṇa dṛḍhena chittvā

4

tataḥ padaṁ tat parimārgitavyaṁ
yasmin gatā na nivartanti bhūyaḥ
tam eva cā 'dyaṁ puruṣaṁ prapadye
yataḥ pravṛttiḥ prasṛtā purāṇī

5

nirmānamohā jitasaṅgadoṣā
adhyātmanityā vinivṛttakāmāḥ
dvandvair vimuktāḥ sukhaduḥkhasaṁjñair
gacchanty amūḍhāḥ padam avyayaṁ tat

1

the gracious lord said:
root above, branches below, the aswattha,* they tell of,
imperishable, of which the chhandas are the leaves; who
knows this, he is a veda knower.

2

below and above, extend its branches, guna-nourished,
sense-objects for twigs;
and below its roots stretch, binding in karma the world
of men.

3

not its form,† either, is here perceived, not its end, nor
beginning, and neither its foundation.
this aswattha, deep-rooted, with the mighty sword
detachment severing,

4

then, let that condition be sought, going where, there is
no returning again;
only to that original purusha surrender, from whom this
ancient world came.

5

without pride, delusion; quelled, the sin attachment;
spiritual always; rid of desire;
liberated from the dualities, called pleasure, pain—the
undeluded go to that state eternal.

---

*peepul tree.
†true form.

6

na tad bhāsayate sūryo
na śaśāṅko na pāvakaḥ
yad gatvā na nivartante
tad dhāma paramaṁ mama

7

màmai 'vā 'ṁśo jīvaloke
jīvabhūtaḥ sanātanaḥ
manaḥṣaṣṭhānī 'ndriyāṇi
prakṛtisthāni karṣati

8.

śarīraṁ yad avāpnoti
yac cā 'py utkrāmatī 'śvaraḥ
gṛhītvai 'tāni saṁyāti
vāyur gandhān ivā 'śayāt

9

śrotraṁ cakṣuḥ sparśanaṁ ca
rasanaṁ ghrāṇam eva ca
adhiṣṭhāya manaś cā 'yaṁ
viṣayān upasevate

10

utkrāmantaṁ sthitaṁ vā 'pi
bhuñjānaṁ vā guṇānvitam
vimūḍhā nā 'nupaśyanti
paśyanti jñānacakṣuṣaḥ

6

not *that* the sun illumines, not moon, not fire;
who go there do not return—that abode supreme, mine.

7

a mere particle of myself, a living spirit, eternal,*
into the world of jivas the senses, mind the sixth,
founded in nature, draws.†

8

a body when assuming, and also when leaving it,
the lord takes all these,
leaving, even as the wind scents from their places.

9

ears, eyes, and touch, taste, and also smell
dwelling in, and mind, *he* the sense-objects enjoys.

10

departing or dwelling, as also experiencing, while
associated with the gunas,
the deluded do not see;** they see who have wisdom's
eye.

---

*becoming.
†to itself.
**the indweller; *it.*

11

yatanto yoginaś cai 'naṁ
paśyanty ātmany avasthitam
yatanto 'py akṛtātmāno
nai 'naṁ paśyanty acetasaḥ

12

yad ādityagataṁ tejo
jagad bhāsayate 'khilam
yac candramasi yac cā 'gnau
tat tejo viddhi māmakam

13

gām āviśya ca bhūtāni
dhārayāmy aham ojasā
puṣṇāmi cau 'ṣadhīḥ sarvāḥ
somo bhūtvā rasātmakaḥ

14

ahaṁ vaiśvānaro bhūtvā
prāṇināṁ deham āśritaḥ
prāṇāpānasamāyuktaḥ
pacāmy annaṁ caturvidham

15

sarvasya cā 'haṁ hṛdi saṁniviṣṭo
mattaḥ smṛtir jñānam apohanaṁ ca
vedaiś ca sarvair aham eva vedyo
vedāntakṛd vedavid eva cā 'ham

11

striving yogis also, that see, in themselves situated;
even striving, the unrestrained do not see it,
unawakened ones.

12

that lustre of the sun, which the whole world illumines,
that in the moon, and that in fire—that light, know, is
mine.

13

and the earth entering, creatures i support with energy;
and nourish all plants, the moon becoming, sapful.

14

i the fire become, in creatures' bodies dwell;
prana, apana, uniting with, digest food, the four kinds.

15

and, of all, i in their hearts am lodged; from me,
memory, wisdom, and their loss;
and in all the vedas, i alone, the known; vedanta's
author, and also the veda-knower, i.

16

dvāv imau puruṣau loke
kṣaraś cā 'kṣara eva ca
kṣaraḥ sarvāṇi bhūtāni
kūṭastho 'kṣara ucyate

17

uttamaḥ puruṣas tv anyaḥ
paramātme 'ty udāhṛtaḥ
yo lokatrayam āviśya
bibharty avyaya īśvaraḥ

18

yasmāt kṣaram atīto 'ham
akṣarād api co 'ttamaḥ
ato 'smi loke vede ca
prathitaḥ puruṣottamaḥ

19

yo mām evam asaṁmūḍho
jānāti puruṣottamam
sa sarvavid bhajati māṁ
sarvabhāvena bhārata

20

iti guhyatamaṁ śāstram
idam uktaṁ mayā 'nagha
etad buddhvā buddhimān syāt
kṛtakṛtyaś ca bhārata

16
and two persons in this world:
the mortal, and also the immortal;
mortal, all creatures;
the unchanging, the immortal called.

17
but the highest being, another, paramatman called,
who the three worlds enters, sustains them, imperishable
god.

18
because the mortal i transcend, and even the immortal surpass,
so, i am, in the world and in the veda, known as purushottama.*

19
who, thus, undeluded, knows me, purushottama,
he, knowing everything, worships me with all his being, bhaarata.

20
thus, this most secret shastra has been taught by me, o sinless; this, understanding, wise he becomes; and all his duty done, bhaarata.

this is the fifteenth canto of the srimad bhagavad gita named purushottama yoga

---

*the supreme person.

canto 16

the way of the distinction between the divine and the demonic qualities

1

śrībhagavān uvāca
abhayaṁ sattvasaṁśuddhir
jñānayogavyavasthitiḥ
dānaṁ damaś ca yajñaś ca
svādhyāyas tapa ārjavam

2

ahiṁsā satyam akrodhas
tyāgaḥ śāntir apaiśunaṁ
dayā bhūteṣv aloluptvaṁ
mārdavaṁ hrīr acāpalam

3

tejaḥ kṣamā dhṛtiḥ śaucam
adroho nā 'timānitā
bhavanti saṁpadaṁ daivīm
abhijātasya bhārata

4

dambho darpo 'timānaś ca
krodhaḥ pāruṣyam eva ca
ajñānaṁ cā 'bhijātasya
pārtha saṁpadam āsurīm

5

daivī saṁpad vimokṣāya
nibandhāyā 'surī matā
mā śucaḥ saṁpadaṁ daivīm
abhijāto 'si pāṇḍava

1

the gracious lord said:
fearlessness, essential purity, in wisdom's yoga steadfastness,
charity and self-control and sacrifices, sacred study, austerity, rectitude;

2

non-violence, honesty, without anger, renunciation, not critical,
mercy for the living, non-covetousness, gentleness, modesty, free of caprice;

3

vitality, forgiveness, fortitude, cleanliness, without malice, without hubris—
the wealth of one with divine nature born, bhaarata.

4

ostentation, arrogance and great conceit, anger, and also violence,
and ignorance—the endowments of those born, partha, demonic.

5

the divine inheritance liberates, the demonic binds, it is thought.
grieve not: you to wealth divine are born, pandava.

6

dvau bhūtasargau loke 'smin
daiva āsura eva ca
daivo vistaraśaḥ prokta
āsuraṁ pārtha me śṛṇu

7

pravṛttiṁ ca nivṛttiṁ ca
janā na vidur āsurāḥ
na śaucaṁ nā 'pi cā 'cāro
na satyaṁ teṣu vidyate

8

asatyam apratiṣṭhaṁ te
jagad āhur anīśvaram
aparasparasaṁbhūtaṁ
kim anyat kāmahaitukam

9

etāṁ dṛṣṭim avaṣṭabhya
naṣṭātmāno 'lpabuddhayaḥ
prabhavanty ugrakarmāṇaḥ
kṣayāya jagato 'hitāḥ

10

kāmam āśritya duṣpūraṁ
dambhamānamadānvitāḥ
mohād gṛhītvā 'sadgrāhān
pravartante 'śucivratāḥ

6

two kinds of being in the world, the divine and also the demonic;
the divine at length have been spoken of; of the demonic, partha, from me hear.

7

neither what to do nor what not to, they know, the demonic;
no purity and neither conduct, no truth, in them found.

8

unreal, un-founded, they say, the world, *god*-less,
of continuing origin, nothing other than lust-begotten.

9

to this view cleaving, lost souls, of small minds,
come forth, of savage deeds, for the destruction of the world: its enemies.

10

to lust surrendered, insatiable; by hypocrisy, arrogance, conceit, possessed;
through delusion seizing fell designs, they act, sworn to evil.

11

cintām aparimeyāṁ ca
pralayāntām upāśritāḥ
kāmopabhogaparamā
etāvad iti niścitāḥ

12

āśāpāśaśatair baddhāḥ
kāmakrodhaparāyaṇāḥ
hante kāmabhogārtham
anyāyenā 'rthasaṁcayān

13

idam adya mayā labdham
imaṁ prāpsye manoratham
idam astī 'dam api me
bhaviṣyati punar dhanam

14

asau mayā hataḥ śatrur
haniṣye cā 'parān api
īśvaro 'ham ahaṁ bhogī
sidho 'haṁ balavān sukhī

15

āḍhyo 'bhijanavān asmi
ko 'nyo 'sti sadṛśo mayā
yakṣye ḍāsyāmi modiṣya
ity ajñānavimohitāḥ

11

and to cares boundless, ending in death, surrendered;
sensual enjoyment the highest:* that this is all
convinced;

12

by desire's bonds, hundreds, bound; to lust, anger,
yielded;
they strive, in order to gratify their desires,
unscrupulously, great wealth to amass.

13

'this, today, by me gained; this heart's desire i will
satisfy;
this, there is, and this, too, i will have:** more wealth.

14

'by me† slain that enemy; and i will kill others, too;
the lord, i; i, the enjoyer; successful, i, strong, happy.

15

'rich, well-born i am; who else is‡ like me?
i will sacrifice, give charity, rejoice!'—thus, by ignorance
deluded.

---

*aim.

**in future.

†already.

‡there.

16

anekacittavibhrāntā
mohajālasamāvṛtāh
prasaktāḥ kāmabhogeṣu
patanti narake 'śucau

17

ātmasaṁbhāvitāḥ stabdhā
dhanamānamadānvitāḥ
yajante nāmayajñais te
dambhenā 'vidhipūrvakam

18

ahaṁkāraṁ balaṁ darpaṁ
kāmaṁ krodhaṁ ca saṁśritāḥ
mām ātmaparadeheṣu
pradviṣanto 'bhyasūyakāḥ

19

tān chaṁ dviṣataḥ krūrān
saṁsāreṣu narādhamān
kṣipāmy ajasram aśubhān
āsurīṣv eva yoniṣu

20

āsurīṁ yonim āpannā
mūḍhā janmani-janmani
mām aprāpyai 'va kaunteya
tato yānty adhamāṁ gatim

16

by countless fancies confounded, in delusion's net ensnared;
addicted to satisfying lusts, they fall into foetid hell.

17

smug with conceit, obdurate,
with wealth's pride intoxicated,
they sacrifice,* in name sacrifice,
with ostentation, disregarding precept.

18

to egotism, force, pride, lust and rage given:
me, in their own and other's bodies,
hating, these envious ones.

19

these, haters vicious, vilest of men, in samsara,
i cast repeatedly only into inauspicious, demon wombs.

20

fiendish wombs finding, the deluded, birth after birth,
me far from attaining, kaunteya, then devolve to the basest state.

---

*only.

21

trividhaṁ narakasye 'daṁ
dvāraṁ nāśanam ātmanaḥ
kāmaḥ krodhas tathā lobhas
tasmād etat trayaṁ tyajet

22

etair vimuktaḥ kaunteya
tamodvārais tribhir naraḥ
ācaraty ātmanaḥ śreyas
tato yāti parāṁ gatiṁ

23

yaḥ śāstravidhim utsṛjya
vartate kāmakārataḥ
na sa siddhim avāpnoti
na sukhaṁ na parāṁ gatim

24

tasmāc chāstraṁ pramāṇaṁ te
kāryākāryavyavasthitau
jñātvā śāstravidhānoktaṁ
karma kartum ihā 'rhasi

21

threefold, of this hell, the gates, which destroy the soul—
lust, anger and greed; so, these three abandon.

22

from these the man who is liberated, kaunteya, gates to darkness, three,
does what is good for his soul, then reaches the supreme condition.

23

who scriptural law forsakes, acts by desire's dictates,
he does not perfection attain, not happiness, not the highest goal.

24

so, let the shastras* be your authority: what may be done, what is forbidden, to determine;
knowing what the scripture's laws declare, your karma you must do, here.†

this is the sixteenth canto of the srimad bhagavad gita named daivaasurasampad vibhaga yoga

---

*scriptures: the vedas, the vedanga/upanishads, the eighteen great puranas. the ramayana and mahabharata are traditionally only considered itihasas, histories.
†in this world.

canto 17

the way of the divisions of the three kinds of faith

1

arjuna uvāca
ye śāstravidhim utsṛjya
yajante śraddhayā 'nvitāḥ
teṣāṁ niṣṭhā tu kā kṛṣṇa
sattvam āho rajas tamaḥ

2

śrībhagavān uvāca
trividhā bhavati śraddhā
dehināṁ sā svabhāvajā
sāttvikī rājasī cai 'va
tāmasī ce 'ti tāṁ śṛṇu

3

sattvānurūpā sarvasya
śraddhā bhavati bhārata
śraddhāmayo 'yaṁ puruṣo
yo yacchraddhaḥ sa eva saḥ

4

yajante sāttvikā devān
yakṣarakṣāṁsi rājasāḥ
pretān bhūtagaṇaṁś cā 'nye
yajante tāmasā janāḥ

5

aśāstravihitaṁ ghoraṁ
tapyante ye tapo janāḥ
dambhāhaṁkārasaṁyuktāḥ
kāmarāgabalānvitāḥ

1

arjuna said:

who scriptural laws forsake, but worship, with faith—
what is their condition, krishna, sattva, rajas or tamas?

2

the gracious lord said:

threefold is the faith of the embodied, of their nature born—
sattvik, rajasik and also tamasik; and hear about it.

3

in concord with his nature everyone's faith is, bhaarata:
of his faith's nature, man—what his faith is, that indeed is he.

4

the sattvikas worship the devas; the rajasas do yakshas and rakshasas;
pretas and other kinds of bhutas, tamasik men worship.

5

not ordained by the shastras, violent austerities those men perform,
to pride, egotism yoked, by lust, passion's force possessed.

6

karśayantaḥ śarīrasthaṁ
bhūtagrāmam acetasaḥ
māṁ cai 'vā 'ntaḥśarīrasthaṁ
tān viddhy āsuraniścayān

7

āhāras tv api sarvasya
trividho bhavati priyaḥ
yajñas tapas tathā dānaṁ
teṣāṁ bhedam imaṁ śṛṇu

8

āyuḥsattvabalārogya-
sukhaprītivivardhanāḥ
rasyāḥ snigdhāḥ sthirā hṛdyā
āhārāḥ sāttvikapriyāḥ

9

kaṭvamlalavaṇātyuṣṇa-
tīkṣṇarūkṣavidāhinaḥ
āhārā rājasasye 'ṣṭā
duḥkhaśokāmayapradāḥ

10

yātayāmaṁ gatarasaṁ
pūti paryuṣitaṁ ca yat
ucchiṣṭam api cā 'medhyaṁ
bhojanaṁ tāmasapriyam

6

torturing the elements in the body, the senseless,
and me, also, dwelling in the body—these, know, of
demonic resolve.

7

the food, too, by all liked, is of three kinds;
sacrifice, austerity, charity, as well;
of the divisions of these, hear.

8

longevity, vitality, strength, health,
happiness, love, which augment;
succulent, soft, nourishing, tasty—foods dear to the
sattvik.

9

bitter, sour, salty, hot, pungent, harsh, burning—
foods by the rajasika liked: pain, grief, disease causing.

10

old, insipid, putrid, stale and what is
refuse and also unclean—food to tamasas dear.

11

aphalākāṅkṣibhir yajño
vidhidṛṣṭo ta ijyate
yaṣṭavyam eve 'ti manaḥ
samādhāya sa sāttvikaḥ

12

abhisaṁdhāya tu phalaṁ
dambhārtham api cai 'va yat
ijyate bharataśreṣṭha
taṁ yajñaṁ viddhi rājasam

13

vidhihīnam asṛṣṭānnaṁ
mantrahīnam adakṣiṇam
śraddhāvirahitaṁ yajñaṁ
tāmasaṁ paricakṣate

14

devadvijaguruprājña-
pūjanaṁ śaucam ārjavam
brahmacaryam ahiṁsā ca
śārīraṁ tapa ucyate

15

anudvegakaraṁ vākyaṁ
satyaṁ priyahitaṁ ca yat
svādhyāyābhyasanaṁ cai 'va
rāṅmayaṁ tapa ucyate

11

by those expecting no reward, the sacrifice
which by scriptural decree is offered,
exclusively as a duty, mind absorbed, that is sattvik.

12

but aiming for its fruit, and also for display, what
is offered, best of bhaaratas, that sacrifice, know, is
rajasik.

13

against law,* where no food is given, without mantras,
without dakshina,†
of faith devoid, the yagna is tamasik, they say.

14

of the gods, the twice-born, gurus, the wise, worship;
purity, rectitude,
continence and non-violence—bodily austerity is called.

15

speech which no offence causes, and which is truthful,
pleasant and benign,
and also regular recitation of the veda—verbal austerity
is called.

---

*scriptural.
†the fee paid to priests.

16

manaḥprasādaḥ saumyatvaṁ
maunam ātmavinigrahaḥ
bhāvasaṁśuddhir ity etat
tapo mānasam ucyate

17

śraddhayā parayā taptaṁ
tapas tat trividhaṁ naraiḥ
aphalākāṅkṣibhir yuktaiḥ
sāttvikaṁ paricakṣate

18

satkāramānapūjārthaṁ
tapo dambhena cai 'va yat
kriyate tad iha proktaṁ
rājasaṁ calam adhruvam

19

mūḍhagrāheṇā 'tmano yat
pīḍayā kriyate tapaḥ
parasyo 'tsādanārthaṁ vā
tat tāmasam udāhṛtam

20

dātavyam iti yad dānaṁ
dīyate 'nupakāriṇe
deśe kāle ca pātre ca
tad dānaṁ sāttvikaṁ smṛtam

16
mental calm, gentleness, silence, self-control,
purity of feeling, all these—austerity of mind are called.

17
with faith transcendent undertaken,
this threefold penance, by men
who wish for no gain, devoted—sattvik is called.

18
for respect, honour, reverence, the austerity,
and which with ostentation
is performed, that, here, is deemed rajasik: fleeting, impermanent.

19
from foolish belief, the self torturing,
the penance that is practised,
or to others meaning harm—that tamasik is said to be.

20
'to give is a duty': thus,* to give charity, without† obligation,
and at a proper time and place—that charity is sattvik regarded.

---

*thinking.
†expecting.

21

yat tu pratyupakārārthaṁ
phalam uddiśya vā punaḥ
dīyate ca parikliṣṭaṁ
tad dānaṁ rājasaṁ smṛtam

22

adeśakāle yad dānam
apātrebhyaś ca dīyate
asatkṛtam avajñātaṁ
tat tāmasam udāhṛtam

23

auṁ tat sad iti nirdeśo
brahmaṇas trividhaḥ smṛtaḥ
brāhmaṇās tena vedāś ca
yajñāś ca vihitāḥ purā

24

tasmād aum ity udāhṛtya
yajñadānatapaḥkriyāḥ
pravartante vidhānoktāḥ
satataṁ brahmavādinām

25

tad ity anabhisaṁdhāya
phalaṁ yajñatapaḥkriyāḥ
dānakriyāś ca vividhāḥ
kriyante mokṣakāṅkṣibhiḥ

21

but that which to be reciprocated,
or aiming for its fruit, in future,
and given grudgingly—that charity rajasik is considered.

22

at the wrong place, time: that charity given,
and to the undeserving,
without respect, contemptuously—that tamasik is told.

23

aum tat sat—this is declared brahman's threefold name:
brahmanas, by this, and the veda and sacrifice, created of old.

24

so, *aum*, thus uttering, acts of sacrifice, charity, austerity
are performed, scripture-enjoined, always by brahmavadis.*

25

tat: thus,** without desiring their fruit,
acts of sacrifice, penance
and various deeds of charity are performed,
by liberation seekers.

---

*expounders, followers of the veda.

**they say.

26

sadbhāve sādhubhāve ca
sad ity etat prayujyate
praśaste karmaṇi tathā
sacchabdaḥ pārtha yujyate

27

yajñe tapasi dāne ca
sthitiḥ sad iti co 'cyate
karma cai 'va tadarthīyaṁ
sad ity evā 'bhidhīyate

28

aśraddhayā hutaṁ dattaṁ
tapas taptaṁ kṛtaṁ ca yat
asad ity ucyate pārtha
na ca tat pretya no iha

26

reality and goodness, *sat* for these is used;
for laudable deeds, as well, the word *sat*, partha, is used.

27

in sacrifice, austerity and charity, constancy—*sat* is called;
and also karma done for *that*, *sat*, indeed, is named.

28

without faith, oblation,* gifts,†, austerity performed, and whatever‡ done,
asat it is called, partha, and is of no account hereafter nor here.

this is the seventeenth canto of the srimad bhagavad gita named sraddhatrai vibhaga yoga

---

*offered.
†given.
‡else

canto 18

the way of renunciation, liberation

1

arjuna uvāca
saṁnyāsasya mahābāho
tattvam icchāmi veditum
tyāgasya ca hṛṣīkeśa
pṛthak keśiniṣūdana

2

śrībhagavān uvāca
kāmyānāṁ karmaṇāṁ nyāsaṁ
saṁnyāsaṁ kavayo viduḥ
sarvakarmaphalatyāgaṁ
prāhus tyāgaṁ vicakṣaṇāḥ

3

tyājyaṁ doṣavad ity eke
karma prāhur manīṣiṇaḥ
yajñadānatapaḥkarma
na tyājyam iti cā 'pare

4

niścayaṁ śṛṇu me tatra
tyāge bharatasattama
tyāgo hi puruṣavyāghra
trividhaḥ saṁprakīrtitaḥ

5

yajñadānatapaḥkarma
na tyājyaṁ kāryam eva tat
yajño dānaṁ tapaś cai 'va
pāvanāni manīṣiṇām

1

arjuna said:

of sannyasa,* mahabaho, the truth i wish to know,
and about tyaga,† hrishikesa,‡ separately, kesinisudana.**

2

the gracious lord said:

desire-impelled karma abandoning, as sannyasa the seers understand;
all karma's fruit sacrificing, call tyaga, the knowing.

3

'renounced as an evil, all karma', say some thinkers;
'acts of sacrifice, charity, austerity must not be abandoned', and so say others.

4

decisively hear from me about this tyaga, best of the bhaaratas;
for, relinquishment, purushavyaghra,# of three kinds is declared.

5

works of sacrifice, charity, penance, these are not to be relinquished but surely performed;
sacrifice, charity and also austerity are purifiers of the wise.

---

*renunciation.
†relinquishment.
‡krishna.
**krishna, vishnu: slayer of the demon kesin.
#best of men; tiger among men.

6

etāny api tu karmāṇi
saṅgaṁ tyaktvā phalāni ca
kartavyānī 'ti me pārtha
niścitaṁ matam uttamam

7

niyatasya tu saṁnyāsaḥ
karmnaṇo no 'papadyate
mohāt tasya parityāgas
tāmasaḥ parikīrtitaḥ

8

duḥkham ity eva yat karma
kāyakleśabhayāt tyajet
sa kṛtvā rājasaṁ tyāgaṁ
nai 'va tyāgaphalaṁ labhet

9

kāryam ity eva yat karma
niyataṁ kriyate 'rjuna
saṅgaṁ tyaktvā phalaṁ cai 'va
sa tyāgaḥ sāttviko mataḥ

10

na dveṣṭy akuśalaṁ karma
kuśale nā 'nuṣajjate
tyāgī sattvasamāviṣṭo
medhāvī chinnasaṁśayaḥ

6

but even these works done, attachment leaving and fruit,
as duty—this, partha, my decided view, the best.

7

but with religious duty, the renunciation of* karma is not proper;
through delusion its abandonment, tamasik is declared.

8

painful: so being, a duty; bodily suffering fearing, if it is abandoned—
he, performing merely a rajasik relinquishment, surely does not relinquishment's fruit gain.

9

when just because it ought to be, a prescribed duty is done, arjuna,
leaving attachment, and also its fruit, that relinquishment is considered sattvik.

10

neither averse to unpleasant karma, nor to pleasant work attached—
the tyagi: of sattva possessed, intelligent, doubts dispelled.

*such.

11

na hi dehabhṛtā śakyaṁ
tyaktuṁ karmāṇy aśesataḥ
yas tu karmaphalatyāgī
sa tyāgī 'ty abhidhīyate

12

aniṣṭam iṣṭaṁ miśraṁ ca
trividhaṁ karmaṇaḥ phalam
bhavaty atyāginām pretya
na tu saṁnyāsināṁ kvacit

13

pañcai 'tāni mahābāho
kāraṇāni nibodha me
sāṁkhye kṛtānte proktāni
siddhaye sarvakarmaṇām

14

adhiṣṭhānaṁ tathā kartā
karaṇaṁ ca pṛthagvidham
vividhāś ca pṛthakceṣṭā
daivaṁ cai 'va 'tra pañcamam

15

śarīravāṅmanobhir yat
karma prārabhate naraḥ
nyāyyaṁ vā viparītaṁ vā
pañcai 'te tasya hetavaḥ

11

surely, impossible, for the embodied to renounce karma entirely;
but who the fruit of karma relinquishes,
he a tyagi is said to be.

12

unpleasant, pleasant and mixed: of three kinds karma's fruit,
accruing to non-relinquishers after death,
but not to sannyasis, ever.

13

these five, mahabaho, causes, learn from me,
in the samkhya doctrine mentioned, for the
accomplishment of all karma.

14

the place and also the doer; and the various actions;
the many and different endeavours; and also destiny,
the fifth of these.

15

with body, speech, mind, whatever karma a man undertakes,
whether just or the opposite, these five are its causes.

16

tatrai 'vaṁ sati kartāram
ātmānaṁ kevalaṁ tu yaḥ
paśyaty akṛtabuddhitvān
na sa paśyati durmatiḥ

17

yasya nā 'haṁkṛto bhāvo
buddhir yasya na lipyate
hatvā 'pi sa imāṁl lokān
na hanti na nibadhyate

18

jñānaṁ jñeyaṁ parijñātā
trividhā karmacodanā
karaṇaṁ karma karte 'ti
trividhaḥ karmasaṁgrahaḥ

19

jñānaṁ karma ca kartā ca
tridhai 'va guṇabhedataḥ
procyate guṇasaṁkhyāne
yathāvac chṛṇu tāny api

20

sarvabhūteṣu yenai 'kaṁ
bhāvam avyayam īkṣate
avibhaktaṁ vibhakteṣu
taj jñānaṁ viddhi sāttvikam

16

this being so, who, yet, as the only doer himself
sees, from ignorance, he does not see: foolish one.

17

who no egotism has, whose intellect is not defiled,
though he kills these men, he neither slays nor is
bound.*

18

knowledge, the known, the knower: the triune impulse
to karma;
the instrument, action, the agent, these the threefold
conjunction of karma.

19

knowledge and action and agent, of three kinds only,
the distinctions of the gunas,
said to be, in the philosophy of the gunas; respectively,
hear, of these, also.

20

in all beings, the knowledge by which the *one*,
imperishable, is seen,
undivided in the divided, that wisdom, know, is sattvik.

---

*by what he does.

21

pṛthaktvena tu yaj jñānaṁ
nānābhāvān pṛthagvidhān
vetti sarveṣu bhūteṣu
taj jñānaṁ viddhi rājasam

22

yat tu kṛtsnavad ekasmin
kārye saktam ahetukam
atattvārthavad alpaṁ ca
tat tāmasam udāhṛtam

23

niyataṁ saṅgarahitam
arāgadveṣataḥ kṛtam
aphalaprepsunā karma
yat tat sāttvikam ucyate

24

yat tu kāmepsunā karma
sāhaṁkāreṇa vā punaḥ
kriyate bahulāyāsaṁ
tad rājasam udāhṛtam

25

anubandhaṁ kṣayaṁ hiṁsām
anapekṣya ca pauruṣam
mohād ārabhyate karma
yat tat tāmasam ucyate

21

but separately, which knowledge, diverse entities, of various kinds,
perceives, in all creatures—that knowledge, know, is rajasik.

22

but what, as the whole, to one effect clings, illogically:
the unreal and trivial, that tamasik is said to be.

23

which, ordained, without attachment, without attraction or aversion is done,
by one not desiring its fruit, that karma is sattvik called.

24

but that karma, prompted by desire, or again, with egotistical motives,
done, with great strain, that is rajasik called.

25

for consequence, loss, violence: disregard, and for capability;
through delusion the karma undertaken, that tamasik is called.

26

muktasaṅgo 'nahaṁvādī
dhṛtyutsāhasamanvitaḥ
siddhyasiddhyor nirvikāraḥ
kartā sāttvika ucyate

27

rāgī karmaphalaprepsur
lubdho hiṁsātmako 'śuciḥ
harṣaśokānvitaḥ kartā
rājasaḥ parikīrlitaḥ

28

ayuktaḥ prākṛtaḥ stabdhaḥ
śaṭho naikṛtiko 'lasaḥ
viṣādī dīrghasūtrī ca
kartā tāmasa ucyate

29

buddher bhedaṁ dhṛteś cai 'va
guṇatas trividhaṁ śṛṇu
procyamānam aśeṣeṇa
pṛthaktvena dhanaṁjaya

30

pravṛttiṁ ca nivṛttiṁ ca
kāryākārye bhayābhaye
bandhaṁ mokṣaṁ ca yā vetti
buddhiḥ sā pārtha sāttvikī

26

free from attachment, not egotistical, of fortitude, zeal, possessed;
by success, failure, unmoved—that doer is sattvik called.

27

passionate, keenly wanting karma's fruit, greedy, violent-minded, impure;
by elation, dejection moved—that agent rajasik is deemed.

28

unstable, feral, obstinate, deceitful, spiteful, lazy;
morose and procrastinating—that doer tamasik is said to be.

29

to the divisions of intellect and also fortitude, according to the gunas, threefold, listen,
told fully, separately, dhananjaya.

30

action and inactivity and what to do, what not to do, fear, fearlessness,
bondage and liberation that intellect which knows, that, partha, is sattvik.

31

yayā dharmam adharmaṁ ca
kāryaṁ cā 'kāryam eva ca
ayathāvat prajānāti
buddhiḥ sā pārtha rājasī

32

adharmaṁ dharmam iti yā
manyate tamasā 'vṛtā
sarvārthān viparītāṁś ca
buddhiḥ sā pārtha tāmasī

33

dhṛtyā yayā dhārayate
manaḥprāṇendriyakriyāḥ
yogenā 'vyabhicāriṇyā
dhṛtiḥ sā pārtha sāttvikī

34

yayā tu dharmakāmārthān
dhṛtyā dhārayate 'rjuna
prasaṅgena phalākāṅkṣī
dhṛtiḥ sā pārtha rājasī

35

yayā svapnaṁ bhayaṁ śokaṁ
viṣādaṁ madam eva ca
na vimuñcati durmedhā
dhṛtiḥ sā pārtha tāmasī

31

by which dharma and adharma, and what to do and also what not to,
is erroneously known—that intellect, partha, rajasik.

32

adharma as dharma that which regards, in darkness shrouded,
and all things pervertedly—that intellect, partha, tamasik.

33

the fortitude by which one rules mind, life breaths, senses' functions,
through yoga unwavering—that firmness, partha, sattvik.

34

but the fortitude by which to dharma, kama, artha one clings, arjuna,
through attachment to the desire for gain*—that firmness, partha, rajasik.

35

by which sleep, fear, sorrow, dejection and also arrogance
a fool does not leave—that obduracy, partha, tamasik.

---

*the fruit of karma.

36

sukhaṁ tv idānīṁ trividhaṁ
śṛṇu me bharatarṣabha
abhyāsād ramate yatra
duḥkhāntaṁ ca nigacchati

37

yat tad agre viṣaṁ iva
pariṇāme 'mṛtopamam
tat sukhaṁ sāttvikaṁ proktam
ātmabuddhiprasādajam

38

viṣayendriyasaṁyogād
yat tad agre 'mṛtopamam
pariṇāme viṣam iva
tat sukhaṁ rājasaṁ smṛtam

39

yad agre cā 'nubandhe ca
sukhaṁ mohanam ātmanaḥ
nidrālasyapramādotthaṁ
tat tāmasam udāhṛtam

40

na tad asti pṛthivyāṁ vā
divi deveṣu vā punaḥ
sattvaṁ prakṛtijair muktaṁ
yad ebhiḥ syāt tribhir guṇaiḥ

36

but of happiness, now, the three kinds, hear from me, bharatarishabha—
long practice through which enjoyed, and sorrow's end attained.

37

that which at first like poison, at the end like amrita,*
that joy sattvika, it's told, of the soul's intelligence,†
serene, born.

38

from contact between objects of sensuality,‡ the senses,
which arises, at first like amrita,
but at the end is like poison—that joy rajasik is called.

39

and which joy, both at first and at the end, binding in delusion the soul,
and which from sleep, sloth, heedlessness arise—that tamasik is deemed.

40

there is not on earth or, again, in heaven among the gods,
a being that is free from these prakriti-born three gunas.

---

*nectar.

†in the sense of realisation, enlightenment.

‡and.

41

brāhmaṇakṣatriyaviśāṁ
śūdrāṇāṁ ca paraṁtapa
karmāṇi pravibhaktāni
svabhāvaprabhavair guṇaiḥ

42

śamo damas tapaḥ śaucaṁ
kṣāntir ārjavam eva ca
jñānaṁ vijñānam āstikyaṁ
brahmakarma svabhāvajam

43

śauryaṁ tejo dhṛtir dākṣyaṁ
yuddhe cā 'py apalāyanam
dānam īśvarabhāvaś ca
kṣātraṁ karma svabhāvajam

44

kṛṣigaurakṣyavāṇijyaṁ
vaiśyakarma svabhāvajam
paricaryātmakaṁ karma
śūdrasyā 'pi svabhāvajam

45

sve-sve karmaṇy abhirataḥ
saṁsiddhiṁ labhate naraḥ
svakarmanirataḥ siddhiṁ
yathā vindati tac chṛṇu

41
of brahmanas, kshatriyas, vaisyas and sudras, parantapa,
their duties are divided, by their innate qualities.

42
serenity, self-control, austerity, purity, forbearance, and
also uprightness;
knowledge, wisdom, belief in *god*—a brahmana's duties,
of his nature born.

43
valour, boldness, fortitude, skill, and even in war not
fleeing;
generosity and lordliness—a kshatriya's duties, of his
nature born.

44
farming, protecting the cow, commerce—a vaisya's
karma, nature born;
karma of the essence of service,
a sudra's, also of his nature born.

45
each to his own duty devoted, man attains perfection;
in his own karma absorbed, how perfection one attains,
that hear.

46

yataḥ pravṛttir bhūtānāṁ
yena sarvam idaṁ tatam
svakarmaṇā tam abhyarcya
siddhiṁ vindati mānavaḥ

47

śreyān svadharmo viguṇaḥ
paradharmāt svanuṣṭhitāt
svabhāvaniyataṁ karma
kurvan nā 'pnoti kilbiṣam

48

sahajaṁ karma kaunteya
sadoṣam api na tyajet
sarvārambhā hi doṣeṇa
dhūmenā 'gnir ivā 'vṛtāḥ

49

asaktabuddhiḥ sarvatra
jitātmā vigataspṛhaḥ
naiṣkarmyasiddhiṁ paramāṁ
saṁnyāsenā 'dhigacchati

50

siddhiṁ prāpto yathā brahma
tathā 'pnoti nibodha me
samāsenai 'va kaunteya
niṣṭhā jñānasya yā parā

46
from *whom* beings arise; *who* all this pervades:
through one's own karma *him* worshipping, perfection a man achieves.

47
better in one's own dharma, imperfectly, than in another's dharma, immaculately;
by one's naturally ordained karma doing, one incurs no sin.

48
the karma one is born to, kaunteya, though flawed, one must not abandon;
for, all endeavours by faults, even as fire by smoke, are clouded.

49
unattached, his intelligence, everywhere; mind conquered; desire gone;
to inaction's perfection supreme, through renunciation, he comes.

50
finding this perfection, brahman, also, how he finds learn from me,
in brief, kaunteya, that consummation of knowledge, transcendent.

51

buddhyā viśuddhayā yukto
dhṛtyā 'tmānaṁ niyamya ca
śabdādīn viṣayāṁs tyaktvā
rāgadveṣau vyudasya ca

52

viviktasevī laghvāśī
yatavākkāyamānasaḥ
dhyānayogaparo nityaṁ
vairāgyaṁ samupāśritaḥ

53

ahaṁkāraṁ balaṁ darpaṁ
kāmaṁ krodhaṁ parigraham
vimucya nirmamaḥ śānto
brahmabhūyāya kalpate

54

brahmabhūtaḥ prasannātmā
na śocati na kāṅkṣati
samaḥ sarveṣu bhūteṣu
madbhaktiṁ labhate paraṁ

55

bhaktyā mām abhijānāti
yāvān yaś cā 'smi tattvataḥ
tato māṁ tattvato jñātvā
viśate tadanantaram

51

with intellect, purified, yoked, and firmly the mind restraining,
sound and objects of sensuality leaving, and likes, dislikes, rejecting;

52

living in solitude, eating little, controlling speech, body, mind;
in dhyana yoga* absorbed, always, in dispassion sheltering;

53

egotism, force, arrogance, lust, anger, possessions,
forsaking, without 'mine', peaceful—to become brahman, he is fit.

54

becoming brahman, soul blissful, he neither sorrows nor desires;
alike to all beings, for me devotion he finds, supreme.

55

through devotion, me, he knows,
how much and what i am, in truth;
then, me truly knowing, he enters into me.

*meditation.

56

sarvakarmāṇy api sadā
kurvāṇo madvyapāśrayaḥ
matprasādād avāpnoti
śāśvataṁ padam avyayam

57

cetasā sarvakarmāṇi
mayi saṁnyasya matparaḥ
buddhiyogam upāśritya
maccittaḥ satataṁ bhava

58

maccittaḥ sarvadurgāṇi
matprasādāt tariṣyasi
atha cet tvam ahaṁkārān
na śroṣyasi vinaṅkṣyasi

59

yad ahaṁkāram āśritya
na yotsya iti manyase
mithyai 'ṣa vyavasāyas te
prakṛtis tvāṁ niyokṣyati

60

svabhāvajena kaunteya
nibaddhaḥ svena karmaṇā
kartuṁ ne 'cchasi yan mohāt
kariṣyasy avaśo 'pi tat

56

even* all karma always doing, in me sheltering,
through my grace, he attains the eternal state, immutable.

57

through thought, all karma to me renouncing; me the ultimate;
to buddhi yoga resorting, on me your heart constantly fix.

58

on me your thought,** all difficulties by my grace you will cross;
but if you, from pride, do not listen, you will perish.

59

if, ego indulging, 'i will not fight', you think:
vain this resolve of yours—your nature will compel you.

60

by your own nature-born karma, kaunteya, bound,
what you do not want to do—being deluded—even that you will do, helplessly.

---

*while; though.

**fixing your thoughts on *me*.

61

īśvaraḥ sarvabhūtānāṁ
hṛddeśe 'rjuna tiṣṭhati
bhrāmayan sarvabhūtāni
yantrārūḍhāni māyayā

62

tam eva śaraṇaṁ gaccha
sarvabhāvena bhārata
tatprasādāt parāṁ śāntiṁ
sthānaṁ prāpsyasi śāśvatam

63

iti te jñānam ākhyātaṁ
guhyād guhyataraṁ mayā
vimṛśyai 'tad aśeṣeṇa
yathe 'cchasi tathā kuru

64

sarvaguhyatamaṁ bhūyaḥ
śṛṇu me paramaṁ vacaḥ
iṣṭo 'si me dṛḍham iti
tato vakṣyāmi te hitam

65

manmanā bhava madbhakto
madyājī māṁ namaskuru
mām evai 'ṣyasi satyaṁ te
pratijāne priyo 'si me

61

god in all beings' hearts, arjuna, dwells,
deluding* all creatures, as† upon a contrivance, with maya.

62

to *him* alone for refuge go, with all your heart, bhaarata;
by his grace, supreme peace you will find, the place eternal.

63

thus, to you, has the wisdom, more secret than secrets, been told by me;
reflect on it fully, and do as you wish.

64

of all, the most secret, again, hear: my supreme word;
since staunchly loved you are by me, so i tell you, for your good.

65

mind** on me; to me be devoted;
to me sacrifice; to me prostrate;
to me you will surely come—truly,
i promise you, who are dear to me.

---

*whirling, spinning, turning around.
†if mounted.
*fix your.

66

sarvadharmān parityajya
mām ekaṁ śaraṇaṁ vraja
ahaṁ tvā sarvapāpebhyo
mokṣayiṣyāmi mā śucaḥ

67

idaṁ te nā 'tapaskāya
nā 'bhaktāya kadācana
na cā 'śuśrūṣave vācyaṁ
na ca māṁ yo 'bhyasūyati

68

ya idaṁ paramaṁ guhyaṁ
madbhakteṣv abhidhāsyati
bhaktiṁ mayi parāṁ kṛtvā
mām evai 'ṣyaty asaṁśayaḥ

69

na ca tasmān manuṣyeṣu
kaścin me priyakṛttamaḥ
bhavitā na ca me tasmād
anyaḥ priyataro bhuvi

70

adhyeṣyate ca ya imaṁ
dharmyaṁ saṁvādam āvayoḥ
jñānayajñena tenā 'ham
iṣṭaḥ syām iti me matiḥ

66

all duty abandoning, to me, the sole refuge, come;
i will liberate you from every sin, do not grieve.

67

this, you must not to the inaustere, not the devotionless, ever,
nor one who has no wish to listen, tell, nor me who derides.

68

who this supreme secret to my devotees teaches,
the highest devotion to me performs, to me surely comes, without doubt.

69

nor is there among men anyone who to me does dearer service than he;
nor will there be than he, to me, another, dearer on earth.

70

and who studies this sacred conversation of ours,
through knowledge's sacrifice, by him, i adored will be—this, my view.

71

śraddhāvān anasūyaś ca
śṛṇuyād api yo naraḥ
so 'pi muktaḥ śubhāṁll lokān
prāpnuyāt puṇyakarmaṇām

72

kaccid etac chrutaṁ pārtha
tvayai 'kāgreṇa cetasā
kaccid ajñānasaṁmohaḥ
praṇaṣṭas te dhanaṁjaya

73

arjuna uvāca
naṣṭo mohaḥ smṛtir labdhā
tvatprasādān mayā 'cyuta
sthito 'smi gatasaṁdehaḥ
kariṣye vacanaṁ tava

74

saṁjaya uvāca
ity ahaṁ vāsudevasya
pārthasya ca mahātmanaḥ
saṁvādam imam aśrauṣam
adbhutaṁ romaharṣaṇam

75

vyāsaprasādāc chrutavān
etad guhyam ahaṁ param
yogaṁ yogeśvarāt kṛṣṇāt
sākṣāt kathayataḥ svayam

71

faithful and without cavil, who just listens, that man:
he, too, liberated, to blessed worlds attains, of those of virtuous deeds.

72

has this been heard, partha, by you, with singular thought?
has your ignorant delusion been dispelled, dhananjaya?

73

arjuna said:
dispelled my delusion, understanding gained, through your grace, achyuta;
i stand firm, doubts gone; i will do as you say.*

74

sanjaya said:
so, i, between vaasudeva and partha, great souls,
this converse heard, wondrous, making my hair standing on end.

75

through vyasa's grace heard i this secret, supreme yoga, from the lord of yoga, krishna, directly, as he told it himself.

---

*your bidding.

76.

rājan saṁsmṛtya-saṁsmṛtya
saṁvādam imam adbhutam
keśavārjunayoḥ puṇyaṁ
hṛṣyāmi ca muhur-muhuḥ

77

tac ca saṁsmṛtya-saṁsmṛtya
rūpam atyadbhutaṁ hareḥ
vismayo me mahān rājan
hṛṣyāmi ca punaḥ-punaḥ

78

yatra yogeśvaraḥ kṛṣṇo
yatra pārtho dhanurdharaḥ
tatra śrīr vijayo bhūtir
dhruvā nītir matir mama

76

o king, i remember, again and again, this wonderful conversation
of kesava, arjuna, sacred, and thrill with joy, over and over.

77

and as i repeatedly recall that *form*, most awesome, of hari,
great my astonishment, o king, and i thrill with joy again and again.

78

where the lord of yoga, krishna, where partha the bowman:
there, fortune, victory, prosperity, eternal justice—this, my belief.

this is the eighteenth canto of the srimad bhagavad gita named moksha sannyasa yoga

aum shanti shanti shanti.
hare krishna.

Appendix

1 Samkhya

Notes directly quoted from Sanskrit-English dictionary of Vaman Shivram Apte:

1. Relating to numbers. 2. Calculating, enumerating. 3. Discriminative. 4. Deliberating, reasoning, a reasoner. 5. Of one of the six systems of Hindu philosophy, attributed to the Sage Kapila. The philosophy is so called because it enumerates twenty-five tattvas or true principles; its chief objective is to enter the final emancipation of the twenty-fifth tattva, the Purusha or Soul, from the bonds of this worldly existence—the fetters of phenomenal creation—by conveying a correct knowledge of the twenty-four other tattvas and by properly discriminating the Soul from them. It regards the whole universe to be a development of an inanimate principle called Prakriti q.v., while the Purusha is altogether passive and simply an onlooker. Samkhya agrees with the Vedanta in being synthetical and thus differs from the analytical Nyaya or Vaiseshika; but its great point of divergence from the Vedanta is that it maintains two principles that Vedanta denies, and it does not admit God as the creator of the universe, which the Vedanta affirms.

2 Yoga

Also from the dictionary of Vaman Shivram Apte:

1. Joining, uniting. 2. Union, conjunction. 3. Deep and abstract meditation, contemplation of the Supreme Spirit. 4. The system of philosophy established by Patanjali, which is considered to be the second division of the Samkhya philosophy, but is practically reckoned as a separate system. The chief aim of the Yoga philosophy is to teach the means by which the human soul may be completely united with the Supreme Spirit and thus secure absolution; and deep abstract meditation is laid down as the chief means to securing this end, elaborate rules being given for the proper practice of such Yoga or concentration of mind.

3. For further details on Samkhya and Yoga philosophy, see:

a. Online article 'Samkhya and Yoga: two classical Hindu 'paths of insight', by Professor Russell Kirkland, University of Georgia.
b. 'Samkhya and Yoga', Encyclopaedia Britannica article.
c. 'Samkhya and Yoga', Wikipedia.
d. *Classical Samkhya and Yoga: The Metaphysics of Experience*, Mikel Burley (Routledge. July 2006).

4. Kalpa

A Note On Hindu Time

'365 human years make one year of the Devas and Pitrs, the Gods and the manes.

Four are the ages in the land of Bharata—the krita, the treta, the dwapara and the kali. The krita yuga lasts 4,800 divine years, the treta 3,600, the dwapara 2,400, and the kali 1,200; and then, another krita yuga begins.

The krita or satya yuga is the age of purity; it is sinless. Dharma, righteousness, is perfect and walks on four feet in the krita. But in the treta yuga, adharma, evil, enters the world and the very fabric of time begins to decay. Finally, the kali yuga, the fourth age, is almost entirely corrupt, with dharma barely surviving, hobbling on one foot.

A chaturyuga, a cycle of four ages, is 12,000 divine years, or 365 x 12,000 human years long. Seventy-one chaturyugas make a manvantara; fourteen manvantaras, a kalpa. A kalpa of 1,000 chaturyugas, twelve million divine years, is one day of Brahma, the Creator.

Eight thousand Brahma years make one Brahma yuga, 1,000 Brahma yugas make a savana, and Brahma's life is 3,003 savanas long. One day of Mahavishnu is the lifetime of Brahma.'

Bibliography

I used *The Concise Sanskrit-English Dictionary* by Vasudeo Govind Apte for this translation, the larger *The Student's Sanskrit-English Dictionary* by Vaman Shivram Apte, the online *Anvaya* of Bhagavadgita.org, as well as the 'synonyms' in Swami Prabhupada's translation.

The actual translations that I consulted, for every *śloka*, were those by Swami Vireswarananda, Dr Sarvapalli Radhakrishnan and Mahatma Gandhi.

The marvellous rendering by Swami Prabhavananda and Christopher Isherwood always resonates in my mind, but I did not refer to it for this work.

ACKNOWLEDGEMENTS

When I began this translation, my Sanskrit (apart from my fair fluency in Hindi and Malayalam) was confined to what I learnt as a young child at home, later in school for a few years, and finally, in my mid-twenties, with the late Sri Parameswara Iyer, who read Kalidasa's *Kumarasambhava* aloud to me and explained it, for all too short a time.

The last was surely my most enjoyable encounter with Sanskrit because by then I myself wanted to listen to and learn the language, and especially for the wonderful personality of my teacher—his faith, gentleness and equanimity, his sense of humour, his wisdom, his humility, personal austerity and his liberality all being unforgettable, particularly when I knew that he lived in straitened circumstances even when he was in his seventies. Of course, there was also his wonderful mastery over Sanskrit, which is a difficult language, and his obvious joy both in the language and the tradition. I owe him a great debt of gratitude.

The late Mr Unnikrishnan, of Palakkad, who also knew Sanskrit, gave me the precious, well-worn copy, which I still have, of Swami Vireswarananda's translation of the *Bhagavad Gita*, published by the Sri Ramakrishna Math. Unnikrishnan, when I met him, made his living as a room waiter at Harrison's Hotel in Madras, where I stayed often during the 1980s and 1990s. He read the Gita every day, for many years, and was a gentle and wise bhakta; you could sense God's grace around him. This translation is also for him.

Finally my late grandfather, Sri K.R.K. Menon, first introduced me to Sanskrit when I was a young boy and he engaged Pavamani Master to teach me. What I owe my grandfather remains beyond calculation, in so many ways.

Other Titles from Ramesh Menon

The Mahabharata: A Modern Rendering (2 Volumes)

The epic is the tale of life—its intrigues, its joys, its sorrows and about the ever elusive truth. The new rendering retells the *Mahabharata* to the contemporary reader in lyrical, modern prose.

Devi: The Devi Bhagavatam Retold

The *Devi Bhagvatam* is a *Shakta Purana* and this is an abridged literary rendering. It is written in the spirit of fervour and abandon which infuses the original and is the hallmark of the worship of the Devi Bhagvatam.

Siva: The Siva Purana Retold

Siva is a vivid retelling of the *Siva Purana* for today's reader. The book contains all the major legends of Siva, bringing them alive for a new generation.

Krishna: Life and Song of the Blue God

The book is a magical, unexpurgated life of Krishna, told in a spirit of bhakti for the modern reader. Never before have Krishna's holy *Gita* (from the *Mahabharata*) and his brilliant, unforgettable life (from the *Bhagavata Purana*) been juxtaposed so vividly and with such enchantment as in this book.

Bhagavata Puraṇa

This book is a full literary rendering of the *Bhagavata Purana*, bringing all the wonder, wisdom and grace of the Book of God to the modern reader. No other Indian scripture claims that it can bestow moksha merely by being heard; but the *Bhagavata Purana* is a living embodiment of the Lord Narayana.

Two Thrillers: The Hunt for K and A Whiff of Old Evil

Two extraordinary thrillers, combining politics, myth and murder mystery in a heady mix. The language is lucid, elegant and powerful.